Dedicated to my crew: Brian, Mason, and Nolan.

contents

PROLOGUE ix

INTRODUCTION
people don't quit organizations;
they quit leaders xv
values first framework xxi

VALUES FIRST
values alignment 3
start with self 17
creating connection 23
more than words 29

AUDIT TIME
stay tuned in 41
this could have been an email 47

LIFE BOUNDARIES
building and keeping boundaries 55
boundaries in transition 63
team boundaries 69

UPLIFTING OTHERS
row, row, row your boat 75

praise for values first teams

"*Values First Teams* is a game-changer for leaders navigating team dynamics in today's fast-paced business world. It's a clear, concise roadm ap to building a culture of trust and alignment."

—Nicole Kalil
PODCAST HOST, *THIS IS WOMAN'S WORK*

"Dr. Laura Eigel's work is essential for uncovering and establishing your personal values, which are foundational for every aspect of life. This theme is elaborated in her insightful first book, *Values First*. Laura has since broadened her practice to include developing and nurturing team values, a critical need in today's environment. Now is the perfect time to explore and implement the practical strategies found in her latest release, *Values First Teams*—a guide on creating a culture attuned for success. Team members crave safety, belonging, achievement, influence, and the chance to make a meaningful contribution at work. I strongly encourage all leaders and team members to read this book to cultivate the vital team culture, connections, and engagement necessary for success."

—Rita Lazar-Tippe
BOARD DIRECTOR, BOARD AND EXECUTIVE DIGITAL ADVISOR

"By guiding leadership teams to center around their values, this book empowers them to foster meaningful engagement and achieve lasting success."

—Renae Slaughter
VICE PRESIDENT TALENT DEVELOPMENT, GLOBAL MANUFACTURING COMPANY

"*Values First Teams* is insightful and immediately applicable. Dr. Laura Eigel's worksheets make the process simple to successfully implement. Her framework can pave the way toward better aligned teams, leading toward increases in both retention and results. We're seeing a revolution when it comes to corporate office culture, and Eigel's publication is incredibly timely."

—Rebecca Swanner

ASSOCIATE PRINCIPAL,
WORKPLACE SECTOR LEADER, HED

"Values-driven leadership isn't just a buzzword—it's a necessity. Laura Eigel provides a proven framework that helps leaders integrate their core beliefs into how they lead and make decisions."

—Alicia Ray

PRINCIPAL CONSULTANT,
BAAR CONSULTING

"A must-read for leaders who want to build high-performing teams without losing sight of what truly matters. Laura Eigel delivers an actionable, practical approach that directly guides leaders through the process of building values-based teams."

—Marilyn Woodruff

DIRECTOR OF TECHNOLOGY,
DAYBRIGHT FINANCIAL

"I wish I had *Values First Teams* years ago. Laura's framework helped me align my values and my leadership style, creating a more engaged and cohesive executive team."

—Christa Swift

FOUNDER AND CEO, C SWIFT SOLUTIONS

LAURA EIGEL, PhD

values
first
teams

how to build a
CULTURE
that's synchronized for
SUCCESS

www.amplifypublishinggroup.com

Values First Teams: How to Build a Culture That's Synchronized for Success

©2025 Laura Eigel, PhD. All Rights Reserved. No part of this publication may be reproduced, stored in a retrieval system or transmitted in any form by any means electronic, mechanical, or photocopying, recording or otherwise without the permission of the author.

Names and identifying characteristics of individuals have been changed. Some dialogue has been recreated.

For more information, please contact:
Amplify Publishing, an imprint of Amplify Publishing Group
620 Herndon Parkway, Suite 220
Herndon, VA 20170
info@amplifypublishing.com

HARDCOVER ISBN: 979-8-89138-481-1
PAPERBACK ISBN: 979-8-89138-744-7

Printed in the United States

uplifting individuals 79
uplifting everyone 85
strategies to grow 91

EXPERIENCING CONFLICT
internal conflict 99
you, me, and conflict makes three 107
leader as navigator 115

SUSTAINING VALUES
moving forward 125
better together 131
getting results you want 135

CONCLUSION
keep rowing and growing 145

VALUES FIRST TEAMS WORKBOOK TOOLS 151
FREQUENTLY ASKED QUESTIONS 155
ACKNOWLEDGMENTS 161
REFERENCES 163

prologue

As an introvert, I've perfected my mental preparation of go-to answers to icebreaker questions for networking events. These answers are cemented in my mind, ready at a moment's notice.

Favorite food? Italian or Mexican.
Cat or dog person? Dog!
Morning or night person? Night.
Coffee or tea? Both, but at different times of the day.
Pancakes or waffles? Either.
Physical book or audiobook? Physical.
Mountain or beach? Beach.

The beach. 100 percent the beach. I want to see the blue hues of the water and watch the sun sink into the horizon line at sunset. The sound of waves is so soothing to me that I fall asleep to it using my sound machine nightly. When I think of the beach, I think about unplanned days. I feel unrushed. I feel paced. I feel present. I connect it to my core values of balance and family.

Growing up in Texas, I remember the summers being hot. Not just "muggy" hot but "breaking into a sweat before you even get to your car" hot. The low temperatures of the day are around eighty degrees Fahrenheit, and it is often still in the high nineties at 9:00 p.m. If you want to enjoy the outdoors, it is most likely at the very beginning of the day or not at all. You spend your time doing indoor activities in the air conditioning until late September when the outdoor temperature starts to become bearable again.

One strategy to escape the heat is to leave. So that's what we did for our family vacation one summer: we traveled to Colorado, where we could wear sweatshirts and pants in July. It was glorious. Not only did we get relief from the heat, but we also got to explore the mountainous geography. Exploring, hiking, and spending time outside with the kids was more meaningful than I could have imagined.

Instead of my usual beach breeze, there was a mountain wind. Instead of the deep blue ocean, there was rocky terrain with terracotta colors and multiple shades of green. Instead of hot, white sand, there were breathtaking views of white peaks. Could the mountains win over the beach? Thankfully, I don't have to choose one over the other. Just like my values have evolved and grown over time, where I find peace has grown too.

In the small mountain town that we visited, there was a picturesque lake. As we walked around the lake's marina, I was immediately drawn to something. Off in the distance was a sign for a rowing club.

In this new environment, I hadn't expected to be able to row on the water. It wasn't on the schedule and not in the plan.

But as soon as I saw the possibility, I knew that I needed to do it. I felt drawn to do it. I reached out to my rowing club and was able to get a letter from my coach to verify my skill level. Within a few days, I was meeting a new rowing club and learning about the lake and their club's safety protocols.

It was the first time that I'd tried rowing on a different lake. Would I be able to do it? Was I good enough to row with a new crew in a different place? Would my skills be up to par? Would I have the confidence? Or would my perfectionism get in my own way like it sometimes does, talking myself out of something so I don't fail?

With all of that swimming around my mind...

I got on the boat in the deepest water I'd ever been in.

I got on the boat with people I'd never rowed with before.

I got on the boat and navigated through water that was unknown to me.

On a crisp early morning, wearing two layers to keep me warm, with the mountains surrounding me, I easily found my place in the quad sculling boat with the crew moving at a relaxed but challenging pace. Hundreds of miles inland and far above the sea level that I usually craved, I found peace.

Through an unexpected experience, I found a way to live my core values of family and balance. I also lived my core value of growth by on-the-water rowing. My trip to Colorado proved once again to me that there is a way to align your values with what you are doing in life.

Wherever you are, you can bring your core values with you. You can prioritize them. You can live them. When I have the chance, I want to say yes to getting on the boat. I want to prioritize it.

While you are in your routine, it is important to live your values. During a transition, moving from one environment to another, it is important to bring them with you wherever you go and experience them wholly. If you are looking, you'll find them where you are.

As a leader, that also means bringing them with you as you grow your career. You'll inevitably be in bigger roles with wider visibility, oftentimes managing a team. You need to bring your values with you there too. Without them, your team culture will be created unintentionally. By leading with your values, you can create the team culture you want.

It's so easy to miss opportunities to live your values—whether you are at work, at home, or in a new environment. You may feel a calling to your values when you least expect it—like on a family vacation in Colorado.

Wherever you are, live your core values.

Get on the boat.

introduction

people don't quit organizations; they quit leaders

The leader of a team casts an important shadow on an individual's work experience. When you don't have the support you need from your leader, it feels isolating, demotivating, and invalidating. I'd argue that it's not just the manager or leader themselves but also the culture that the leader creates that make people quit. I'm not talking about the organizational culture—that's for another book—I'm talking about the team's culture.

If you are a leader, you create a culture. A culture is built no matter what, whether the leader is aware of it or not. The culture is the behavior that you allow. Some leaders create cultures that teams thrive in. Others create toxic environments that team members are just trying to survive. Many leaders aren't being intentional in the cultures they create. When people quit, they quit their managers and the culture that leader has created.

Can you think about a leader that you loved working for? What was it like working for them?

From my own experience, working for a good leader felt challenging but empowering. I felt valued, I contributed beyond my role, and I knew I was making an impact on the department or organization. I felt known and seen by my manager. I felt safe. I felt like I belonged to something bigger than just a role. The culture was absolutely created by my leader. I loved that team, that season of my career. It was truly special.

In my twenty-year career in human resources, I've seen many different types of managers and cultures. I started studying leadership and culture in my doctoral training as an organizational psychologist. I've facilitated team interventions and helped leaders build their visions and team strategies. I've built team culture in the teams that I've led: small teams of two direct reports all the way to an entire global department. Now within the work that I do at my company, The Catch Group (TheCatchGroup.com), I get a front-row seat to team cultures of all sizes, from small businesses to Fortune 500 companies. I can't say that I've seen it all, but I've seen a lot.

This book was never part of a broader career strategy. I wish I could tell you that it was, but I didn't have any intention of writing it. When I sat down to write my debut book, *Values First: How Knowing Your Core Beliefs Can Get You the Life and Career You Want,* I didn't know if I could finish one book, let alone two! But I knew the content I'd developed over decades of experience was important to help change corporate culture. That first book was impactful, winning awards and garnering five-star reviews. Since it's come out, I've coached countless senior and C-suite leaders with the Values First Framework in individual and group coaching sessions. I've seen firsthand as they've utilized the tools to gain clarity, make big career decisions, and build and keep big boundaries.

As these senior leaders advanced in their roles, I partnered with them to implement the Values First Framework within their organizations. I began utilizing the exercises I built for individuals within team settings. The framework worked there too, and it worked well, but for different reasons.

Leaders who used the Values First Framework with their teams have created values-based cultures with behaviors aligned with those values. They built rewards and recognition programs aligned with values. They used values to interview new team members to ensure values alignment. They created work processes and ways of communication that are aligned with the values of their teams.

They created team cultures where leaders feel seen and valued. Cultures where teams hold each member accountable for their behaviors and values. Where they can hold their leader accountable too. And they've done it while also meeting and exceeding business results. Funny how that happens, huh? The reason this book exists is because the Values First Framework works. It's worked for hundreds of individual leaders and their teams, and it can work for your team too.

This book can help you build a values-based culture without sacrificing results. It's for leaders:

- With new teams
- With existing teams
- With growing teams
- With high-performing teams
- With one direct report
- Who create belonging
- Who lead turnarounds
- Who are just beginning their journeys
- Who are in the messy middle
- Who want to leave a legacy near the end of their careers
- Who know who they are at their core
- Who are still figuring out their leadership style
- Who lead companies with thousands of employees

- Who want to lead in new ways that are different from how they've been led in the past
- Who want more than just achieving and exceeding business results
- Who care about how they achieve results

I will be sharing my personal experience with building values-based cultures throughout this book. You will read about examples of my clients who utilize the Values First Framework in their teams to build their team cultures. We'll highlight experiences from different industries, different team sizes, and different levels within organizations.

As Lola Bakare, award-winning inclusive marketing strategist, CMO advisor, and founder of be/co, explains of her work, "I don't meet people where they are, I lead them to where they need to be. Why would I go where they are when they can come to me?" You've done the work to get here; you've come this far. It is up to you to get what you need most of it.

Some of the exercises in the book are foundational, while others may be used for teams that are further in their culture-building journey. Take what you need and utilize the tools that feel right for your team size, but also stretch your leadership and try out exercises with a growth mindset.

As you start this work, I encourage you to begin with *Values First: How Knowing Your Core Beliefs Can Get You the Life and Career You Want*. Do the exercises in the Values First Workbook before you dig into the content in this book. I promise, you'll be more prepared and more committed to following through with your team when you do. But it isn't mandatory, and certainly I won't know if you skip it (but you shouldn't skip it!). In this book, I will highlight exercises from *Values First* to come back to with an individual lens and a team lens. You are your team's guide through this process.

I am action oriented, and I have a feeling you are too. This book was created so you can get actionable takeaways to build an intentional team culture. "Intention" is the key word here. You are busy. You know this; I know this. Ensure that you not only digest this content, but intentionally implement the most important actions for you and your team.

I've made it easy for you to take action with the Values First Teams Workbook. The workbook is written for you as a leader to bring your team through exercises using the Values First Framework. Take a minute now to download the Values First Teams Workbook at TheCatchGroup.com/ValuesFirstTeams.

I also offer support for you on my website and in my podcast, *You Belong in the C-Suite*. You can find multiple resources to support your journey to become a values-driven leader at TheCatchGroup.com.

I wholeheartedly believe that a leader builds the culture of their team, whether they are intentional about it or not. The culture is built based on the behaviors that they allow, reward, model, and incentivize—whether they are paying attention to those things or not. I hope this book helps you recognize that you can build your team culture with intention. When you prioritize that work, you will see the benefit of not just the actual business results you get but *how* you get those results.

I know this book will be the tool you need to continue your values journey. I'm excited to help you grow as a leader and guide you in building your team's culture. Let's get started together with a review of the foundation: the Values First Framework.

values first framework

As my nine-year-old says, "Practice makes progress."

When I was a kid, I was told that practice makes perfect. But perfection is unattainable. It keeps us from learning and growing. Perfection has stopped me from starting too many things, anchored by a fear of failure. If I don't start it, then I can't fail at it. Striving for perfection has stopped me from growth. Instead of being the perfect leader, try to become a better leader today than you were yesterday. We are all in progress, but we can get better. That's where the Values First Framework comes in—this framework has intentionality baked into it.

I've been using the Values First Framework with individuals and in organizations since 2021, and a version of it for longer than that through coaching clients and in my own leadership style. I have firsthand knowledge of the power of the framework for individuals, teams, and organizations. The Values First Framework is for more than individuals. It starts with an individual: a people-centered leader that knows what they stand for and is aligned with their values. Maybe they haven't been as intentional as they'd like to be with their time, energy, or team. Maybe they haven't realized how much their behavior can really impact their team. In *Values First Teams*, we explore the impact that your individual leadership can have within your team and your overall organization. We'll broaden the use of the Values First Framework to teams and organizations.

To help you remember the sections of the framework, I've created an acronym: V.A.L.U.E.S. Here's what you'll accomplish in each section of this book using the Values First Framework:

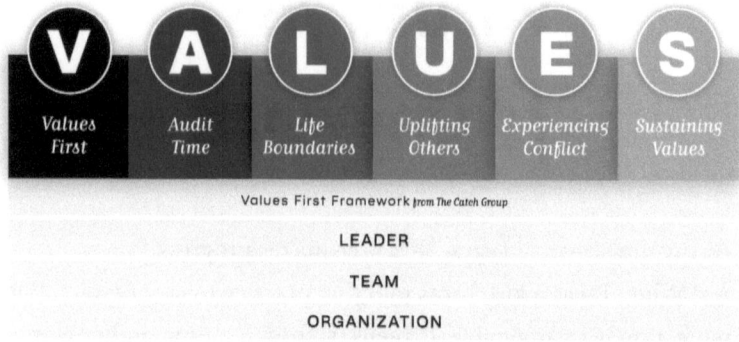

Values First Framework from The Catch Group

LEADER

TEAM

ORGANIZATION

Values First: Dig into what matters most to you and the members of your team to build your team values. You'll gain clarity on values for your team and an understanding of what living those values looks like for the team. You'll learn how to:

- Know when you have values alignment and how to build it for your team
- Build your Values Statement
- Build team connection through values
- Connect your core values to organizational values
- Create team values and behaviors

Audit Time: Audit how your team is currently living up to those values and behaviors. Review the time, energy, systems, and processes your team uses and align them with the team's values. You learn how to:

- Audit the team's strengths and gaps in living values and behaviors
- Assess the team's meeting culture
- Align the systems, processes, and communications with the team's values

Life Boundaries: Establish boundaries to care for team values and set the priorities and accountabilities. You'll learn how to:

- Prioritize and model your own boundaries to empower your team
- Build team boundaries aligned with team values
- Hold each other accountable for the culture you want

Uplifting Others: Build the support you and your team need to live their values, including modeling behaviors, rewards, and recognition. You'll learn how to:

- Uplift individuals by prioritizing connection
- Incentivize team values and behaviors to celebrate the team through recognition
- Utilize strategies to prioritize your team's development

Experiencing Conflict: Design how your team will resolve conflict, give feedback, and move forward in alignment with team values. You'll learn how to:

- Use your core values to resolve internal conflict
- Identify sources of conflict between you and others
- Mediate conflict within your team through team values

Sustaining Values: Build an action plan to intentionally sustain your team culture for the long term. You'll learn how to:

- Prioritize the right actions for the team
- Ensure individual commitment from each team member
- Revisit team values intentionally over time

You'll be able to model your own values and connect back to the organization's values while also tapping into the values of the individuals that belong to your team. Your team values will be a roadmap for you and the group to set expectations, make decisions, prioritize the right work, and reward and motivate everyone. It isn't about the end result; it is about how to get those results. Your values will guide the way you work with your team.

It is about intentionally building the team culture to get the results you want.

You'll be able to build your Values First Team to:

- Hire the best people with high values alignment to your team and organization
- Align an existing team
- Set expectations and hold your team accountable
- Guide decision-making, strategy, and prioritization
- Reward behaviors that get not only results, but get results through team values
- Maintain an engaged, high-performing workforce

Building a Values First Team can give the team clarity of expectations, which leads to big results.

How can your values impact a team or culture? Let's start with that important question.

.

values first

Dig into what matters most to you and the members of your team. You'll build values for your team with behaviors on what living those values looks like for them.

Values First Teams Workbook tools in this section:

- Values Worksheet
- Values Check-In
- Values Alignment Worksheet
- Values Statement Worksheet
- Building Team Connection Tool Kit
- Team Values Worksheet

values alignment

Returning to work after having my first child was rough. I had a three-and-a-half-month maternity leave, which felt like not nearly enough time with our newborn. I was disconnected from my body and mind. I'm sure parents and caregivers can relate.

I convinced my friend Hayley to try a new workout studio with me. I barely made it through and absolutely did not want to return, but Hayley was hooked and convinced me to not give up. Soon we were at our second class, then our third, and then beyond.

The workout studio is where I fell in love with indoor rowing and the way it connected me to my mind and body while honoring my core value of balance.

As with any new skill, I had to first learn the technique of rowing. Although no one part of the stroke is more important than another, we had to start somewhere. I start at the finish position, where my arms extend, floating out from my chest. Next, my torso hinges forward like the hand of a clock and moves to the one o' clock position. Then, with a softening of my knees, I slide into the catch position. This is the moment I prepare to begin the next stroke. I drive back with my legs, bracing my torso as it ticks back into the eleven o' clock position on the clock. My arms draw back into my chest, completing the stroke and returning to where we started: the finish position. There is no real stopping point, however, as the stroke moves continually, much like an infinity symbol has no end.

The repetition of the stroke, that consistency, is when I could let go of all other thoughts and just be in the moment. I hadn't felt that way in a long time, or maybe hadn't ever felt that. Every time I finished a stroke, there was a small recovery as my arms floated away from my body and I slid toward the catch. No rests, no pauses, but a small recovery before the moment of connection at the catch once again. The catch is just before the change of direction. The moment before you drive back with the power of your legs, lats, and torso.

A moment of connection, then a chance to start again with each new stroke. Rowing became such an important symbol for me that I named my company The Catch Group as a reminder of my core values.

In rowing, I was aligned with my values as an individual: balance and achievement. I was also part of a bigger community, a team, that showed up for each other with shared values. That synchronicity between the individuals and the team isn't an accident; it is alignment.

In that workout studio I nearly didn't return to, I found the type of values alignment I'd been craving my entire life.

In this section of the framework, Values First, you'll learn how to:
- Understand when you have values alignment
- Craft values alignment in your team
- Build your Values Statement
- Connect your core values to organizational values
- Create team values and behaviors

Values are a great connector because values are accessible to everyone, like languages you can use to communicate. Values can also be created for different groups, going beyond individual values. You can have team values, department values, and organizational values. Values at different levels or for different-sized groups can exist at the same time. They may not all be in harmony at the same time, but they do coexist. In fact, they often overlap.

I've experienced workplace cultures in a lot of ways. As a student and employee, I've experienced the cultures as a part of organizations. I've experienced the cultures of small consulting firms and global Fortune 50 companies. As an executive coach and consultant, I've also helped leaders navigate through their own workplace cultures and facilitated senior leaders in building their values-based cultures.

A company's culture—or what is most important to them and their shared beliefs and behaviors—is sometimes expressed very explicitly with values, principles, and words that describe what's important. You see these words and phrases on external websites, in new employee orientation, and even printed on company swag. You also feel and experience a company's culture: the unwritten rules and expectations of how they do things.

Oftentimes, as we try to find the best people to work within our organizations, we use the phrase "looking for the best cultural fit." We try to find people that fit within our established company culture. When we find those people, they will be the ones that thrive best there.

What is a culture fit? Culture fit, or person-culture fit, is the relationship between organizational values and individual personality and values. It has been studied for decades. The more congruence between an organization and person, the higher their job satisfaction and organizational commitment.[1] The term "culture fit" has become a popular term in the corporate lexicon, along with so many other terms and phrases like "bandwidth" and "let's circle back on that" that we can't escape. Within corporate speak, the concept of "culture fit" has broadened and been overused.

Here's my hot take: **I think using "culture fit" is problematic.** It doesn't get us what we need at work, for organizations or as employees. And it is doing you a disservice as a leader. It is stalling your real intent, and it is keeping you from what you really want: a high-performing team that's connected to the mission and values of your organization.

Culture fit is often associated with someone that fits within the organizational culture so that they feel like part of the team. Someone who "gets us" or "gets it." As one leader I used to work with said, "I know it when I see it, or rather, I really know when there isn't a culture fit; it feels off."

Culture fit has become a catchall phrase that we use to justify many decisions that we don't know how to specifically express. A "lack of culture fit" is a phrase we use when we are describing why someone who doesn't quite feel like they belong in the organization (even when they have an amazing resume and more than the experience we are looking for). Culture fit is a description and catchall that leaders use to avoid giving specific feedback. It sounds like, "She's just not the right culture fit for the team. She has some great experience, but she didn't really click with the team."

Or "He builds immediate rapport with others, he's got the drive we want, and he fits with the culture. I'm sure he can learn the technical aspects."

Or "I can't put my finger on it, but in meetings they don't seem to get it. They've been here for over three months now, and they aren't getting the culture."

What specifically is the person doing or not doing? What about the culture isn't a fit? What are the specific behaviors you are looking for?

Using "culture fit" as a reason for any decision is a way for conscious and unconscious bias to show up in the decisions that we make at work. Culture fit is being used by organizations to say, "This person isn't like me" or "This person isn't like us." By being intentional with your values, you can mitigate some of this bias.

When you hear the term "culture fit," I want that to be a warning flag to you to dig deeper. I want you to ask more questions.

Using "culture fit" is a warning sign that we aren't digging enough into what it is. When you get a bad vibe from someone in an interview, is it because of something that they are doing that is different than your way? When you get a good feeling from someone, is it because they remind you of yourself?

Using culture fit is too broad of a bucket; it is too easy of an excuse to use instead of articulating the reason at the root of the problem.

Instead of culture fit, I want you to utilize specific attributes of your culture and the behaviors associated with it. I want you to start thinking about the values of your culture, the behaviors associated with those values, and how the values and behaviors of the individual align with the company.

I want you to think about values alignment, not culture fit.

Through her work on *Atlas of the Heart*, Brené Brown unpacks eighty-seven different emotions and feelings. She was surprised by the research findings she had while studying belonging. In her research, the opposite of belonging is fitting in.[2]

She theorizes that we try and fit in because we want to belong to a group or a company. In doing so, we change who we are to fit into this culture. We want to fit. We change ourselves. We compromise ourselves, our identities, our appearance, maybe even our values to fit in. We aren't meeting our need for belonging.

Instead, I want you to ground yourself in your own values and find alignment with an environment that matches your values. The goal is values alignment, not culture fit.

In the Values First Framework, there are values at three different levels:

- Individual or leader level
- Team level
- Organizational level

The overlap of individual and team/organizational values is

values alignment. Think about the values of a group you belong to: maybe a university, an industry group, or a group of individuals with whom you share a common goal. A common experience or a shared set of beliefs and traditions may exist within that group.

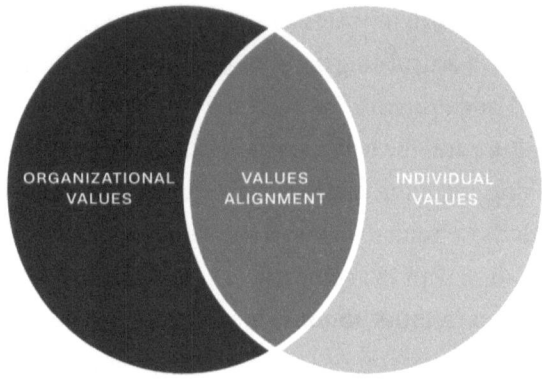

I've belonged to many different groups. I've been in orchestras where creativity and discipline were valued. I've been a part of the Girl Scouts where leadership, collaboration, and learning were valued. I've been a part of schools where honesty, academic excellence, and volunteerism were valued. As I started my consulting and corporate career, I've been a part of organizations where cultures of "drive for results," "truth and candor," and "well-being" were valued. These values say a lot about the culture of a group or organization. They are the written and unwritten rules of what matters in these groups and how they get things done.

Think back to a group you are a part of. You may resonate with the values of that group because they overlap with some of your own core values. Within the Values First Framework, first and most central, are your individual values. That's what matters most to you, the things that are of central importance to you as a leader, a person, and a human. I think your values should overlap with the values you set for your team and overlap with values of the organization you work for.

There should be overlap, and that overlap is called values alignment. We are looking for some percentage of alignment. I don't think those circles ever fully align with each other. You are an individual that cares about a lot of things, and all of those things don't have to overlap with work.

There should be enough overlap to align with what motivates you, what resonates with you. As you join an organization, if you are in alignment with those values—your core values with the organizational values—then you have values alignment. You aren't squeezing or shrinking or changing yourself to fit inside of the organization's circle. You have commonalities. You have values alignment.

But this takes work: you need to know your values. The organization needs to know theirs.

You know what's important to you. You should seek that out in an organization.

To do that, both individuals and organizations need to do a better job in defining their cultures and values. We need to do better at articulating behaviors tied to our cultures. We need to do a better job of recognizing behaviors aligned with our values.

COMMON MISTAKES ORGANIZATIONS MAKE IN VALUES ALIGNMENT

I most commonly see two mistakes that organizations make in this work:

- Organizations haven't done as much culture work as they think
- What companies say and what they do don't match

First, they haven't done as much culture work as they think. They have beautiful company values that are in big, beautiful fonts on posters on their company walls and on the screen savers of every employee's laptop, but they are just words. Their organizational values aren't that specific.

I was listening to a podcast about a show on HGTV, and the host said that he hated the "words on walls" trend that has become so popular. You know the wooden boards that say "live, laugh, love" or the signs that are hung in kitchens that say "gather" or "eat" or simply "kitchen"? The host of the podcast said that he didn't like those as art in homes and made the point that "of course you eat in a kitchen—why do we need to be reminded of that?"

If you bring that perspective into the corporate art space, you see it too. These words on walls in an office environment are meant to be reminders of what's important to the company. This makes them accessible, and employees link back to them in meetings. The words may appear on your company badge or in your company's marketing. I love the idea around these things, to remind you of what the organization stands for and what they want to be. But often, that's where the company's work stops. They talk about the words that are important, maybe with a one- or two-sentence description. And that's it. They don't follow that up with their behaviors. How do these values show up in meetings? How do we get things done?

It is aspiration rather than action. When companies describe their organizational culture, they are often describing their ideal, aspirational culture, not the current one. It is misleading and causes discrepancies for the teams and employees within the organization.

Undefined organizational values can contribute to and exacerbate values misalignment for an individual. If you don't know what's most important to the company you work for, it's hard to understand how your values overlap. Not only do companies need to define their values; they need to do it with specificity.

Values misalignment shows up as conflict or a point of tension for the employee. In the Venn diagram, values misalignment would be illustrated as an organizational value and an individual core value that do not overlap. No commonalities whatsoever.

I've done values clarity work with hundreds of leaders and numerous organizations, and I know that two people can have the same values that may mean completely different things to them individually. The behaviors that they associate with the values are different. If values aren't specific, then there will be multiple interpretations that may conflict with each other.

The second big mistake I see organizations make is that they aren't utilizing the work that they have done on their culture. What does this look like at organizations?

- Not holding people accountable
- Not incentivizing right behaviors
- Incentivizing wrong behaviors
- Not connecting values to the company's strategy

Even if you have values and behaviors, if you don't hold people accountable and incentivize and reward people on those values and behaviors, then you just have words on walls. You also could have a toxic culture. Saying one thing and rewarding another.

Here's an example of saying one thing and doing another. I once worked with a company that valued collaboration. There was training on collaboration, and in it they showed how they did it: working together is better than doing it alone.

When it came to rewards and recognition, often individuals got rewarded based on heroics and something that they did on their own. A leader would be publicly recognized at a company event for going above and beyond in an individual task or a heroic personal effort. Collaboration wasn't rewarded; individual effort was.

What did that promote? It promoted a culture of individual effort in going above and beyond. So even though this company said that the culture was of collaboration, it really wasn't. They were a culture guided by what they rewarded.

CULTURE IS WHAT YOU INCENTIVIZE

I want you to incentivize the behaviors that align with your team's values.

To do that, programs and systems sometimes need to change. New behaviors need to be identified. Employees need to be managed through the changes across the organization. I work with companies that do intentional work to prioritize their values-based cultures. They work with me to look at their organizational values and partner with cross-functional workgroups and senior leaders.

This work is often done when:

- There is a new leader in a team or organization
- When a company has merged two cultures
- When a company truly wants to start incentivizing the right behaviors, tied to what matters most
- Companies are doing culture stuff well, but want to get even better at it

Companies that prioritize their culture arrange time and budgetary allocations to be spent on it. It isn't a nice-to-have. It is a must. Defined, specific organizational values can serve as a filter for organizations to make decisions. In fact, organizations that use their values are more successful.[3]

There's work to do as leaders within these organizations, a responsibility each leader has to their own group.

HOW CAN YOUR LEADERSHIP IMPACT THE ORGANIZATIONAL CULTURE MOST?

You can use your leadership to impact the organization by building team values. You can look at your company's values and further define them with your team. What behaviors or ways of working truly tie to your core values?

As a leader and manager, your role is incredibly important to employees and direct reports. An employee's view of their organization is tied to their perception of their manager. Furthermore, an employee's everyday experience is also tied to their experience with their direct manager.[4] The team culture that you build and how you lead can dramatically impact an employee's experience and overall engagement with their job and the organization.

You have a chance to create the team culture that motivates and inspires the team to do their best work. You can influence the values alignment of the people on your team. I'm inviting you to intentionally build that culture.

A team culture will exist whether you intentionally build it or not. Build the one you want.

This book has "teams" directly in the title, so it is not an accident that I will often have you go through an exercise of self-reflection before you do an exercise with your team. Before you can impact others, you need to be able to look in the mirror and start with the person staring back at you. To help you in your learning journey, I'll note which exercises are for individual self-reflection with a solo rowing icon and which exercises should be done with the team in the same metaphorical boat with a crew rowing icon.

To build the culture you want, let's start with your individual values and identify your Values First.

🏃 INDIVIDUAL REFLECTION

Pause now and download the Values First Teams Workbook at TheCatchGroup.com/ValuesFirstTeams. In it, you'll find the Values Worksheet, which will help you identify your core values.

If you already know your core values, then now is a great time to do a Values Check-In to review your values and celebrate your recent wins or recalibrate what's truly important to you. I've made it easy for you and put these exercises in your Values First Teams Workbook.

Whether this is the first time you've clarified your core values or you are a seasoned Values First pro and you ground yourself in your values often, I know you'll find a new insight through this reflection.

🏃 INDIVIDUAL REFLECTION

Next, I want you to go even further and evaluate your own Values Alignment. You can continue your self-reflection using your Values Alignment Worksheet in your workbook to answer the following questions:

1. How do your core values overlap with your organization's values?
2. What similarities do you see between the organization's values and your own values?

After debriefing this exercise with countless teams and leaders, it isn't uncommon to see similarities between your values and the organization's values. You work where you work for a reason. There may be an overt overlap between your values and the company's values. Or it could be more subtle, with some of your values being reflected in the behavior or language that describes an organizational value.

The amount of overlap doesn't equate to the amount of

fulfillment you are presently feeling with your company. You may align highly with the values your company touts on their external website, even though you have an insider's experience that runs in opposition to outward appearance. You may have been less aligned when you started working with the company, but over time you've seen the company's values show up in different ways, and that has increased your own values alignment over time.

Regardless of the current amount of overlap between your values and the organization's, it is a meaningful data point. If your values aren't overlapping very much, that may be a very acute data point to consider. For many, the overlap will highlight how you connect to the larger organization and be an indicator of your own engagement with your work and company.

Next, we'll talk about how you can use your values to find alignment in important career milestones and inspire others to do the same. You'll hear from Scarlet, who used her values to author her next career move.

start with self

Scarlet is a voracious reader and lifelong learner, which helps her to be self-aware and grounded in her values. However, like many of us, she spreads herself too thin by simultaneously serving on four nonprofit boards and being unable to sit still long enough to read one of the many books she has going. She's always learning and always serving others, which aligns with some of her values but ignores others.

Scarlet and I met while I was a guest speaker for an industry group for female executives where I helped them utilize their values to guide their careers and teams. Scarlet was a C-suite leader looking to align her values with her career opportunities. She came to the talk and loved it, so she signed up for another workshop with me on how to build boundaries and then joined my six-month group coaching program.

During her coaching onboarding, she told me that one of her goals was to show up more authentically in interviews. Before each interview, she felt like she had to spend so much time "doing her homework" to learn about the company and figure out how to communicate her career experience.

"What if you take less time prepping for interviews?" I asked.

"Then I won't feel as confident or ready for the questions they ask me," she said.

"What if you felt confident in other ways?" I questioned. I explained that, in my experience, companies interviewing for roles at her level would want to know about her leadership rather than only her competence. I continued, "You are the expert in your experience and your resume. You know what you've accomplished. I would love for you to feel as confident talking about your leadership style as you do talking about your experience. What would that feel like?"

"It would feel really good," she replied. "I want to be able to work in a culture that values my leadership style. I can do any of these roles. I want to do it in a place where they value me and where I can lead in alignment with my values with integrity and authenticity."

That's the goal I want for all of us: for you and every member of your team.

After our first call, I gave Scarlet the homework of building her Values Statement, something you'll also get to do. A Values Statement is a concise statement about how you lead and what's important to you. It is a leadership elevator speech. You describe your leadership style based on your values. Being able to describe how you lead and what's important to you is a skill. It is a skill you can improve with practice.

Think about leaders that you've loved working for in the past. How would you describe them?

You may think about how they were available to you, how they listened to you, and how they respected your thoughts and ideas. Maybe you'll think about the way they gave you visibility.

I remember one senior leader that I worked for, Shannon. She gave me opportunities to learn, knew what she wanted, was compassionate but tough, told me the truth, and also showed empathy. If I had to guess what her values were, I would guess family, development, honesty, innovation, and adventure. She never told me those were her values, but she showed them to her team. More importantly, she did so in a consistent way. She was the same leader in a one-on-one meeting as she was when presenting to the chief executive officer (CEO) of the company. She was consistent. You always knew where you stood with her, and she had great boundaries. She took her vacations and spent time with her daughters and grandchildren. She was transparent in her leadership and modeled the importance of prioritizing family.

I don't know if Shannon was intentional with building a Values Statement or if it was something she was naturally good at. The consistency of her messages was incredibly helpful and grounding to me as part of her team. It showed the team how she made decisions, it helped us meet her expectations, and it exhibited to us what was important to her.

You may not realize it, but you already have the foundation of your own Values Statement. A Values Statement consists of two main building blocks: first, your core values, and second, behaviors associated with those values. Some of those behaviors may be boundaries that you have or actions that are associated with those values.

I've made it easy for you to build your own Values Statement. Here's the formula:

Values Statement = three core values + behaviors aligned with those values

When I introduce myself when speaking to new audiences, I utilize my Values Statement: "I'm a leader that lives a life and career of my values. I value growth, development, and advocacy. I do this by coaching individuals and organizations to bring more diversity and authenticity into the workplace."

Here's another example of a Values Statement from a leader in my Values First Leader workshop: "I'm a leader that values people—both in serving others and meeting organizational needs—and in enjoying our work while we do it! I do this by listening deeply, adjusting to meet the needs of the person or moment, and focusing on the right work at the right time."

🏃 INDIVIDUAL REFLECTION

Now it is your turn to build your Values Statement. Go to your Values First Teams Workbook to get the Values Statement Worksheet to build your own.

Scarlet built her Values Statement and received feedback from her peers in group coaching. She decided that she would put it into practice right away in her interviews. In our next group coaching meeting, she debriefed us after she used it.

"It was so conversational. It was a different kind of interview. It was less about my previous experience and more about how I got results. I was able to use my Values Statement."

"How did you feel about the interview?" a fellow group coaching participant asked.

"I feel really good about it. I was also able to ask deeper and more intentional questions about the company. From what I've seen I think it could be a really good fit. We'll see though—you never know," she said in a cautiously optimistic tone.

Scarlet ended up accepting a position at that company. When a new team member asked what her values were, she was confidently able to answer that question.

What are the ways you can utilize your Values Statement within your role?

- Interview process
- One-on-one with direct report or stakeholder
- Coffee chat
- Mentoring meeting
- Town hall
- Career discussion
- Project kickoff meeting
- Team or department meeting
- Team off-site

I distinctly remember one conversation I had with a peer at the beginning of the pandemic when I was sharing my availability for our next meeting and reminding him of my working hours. As our Teams call was ending he said, "I love that you are talking about your work-life balance so much right now. It is important."

I replied, "Oh no. I don't have work-life balance. We are barely making it over here. I do have new working hours that I've put in place because of virtual school for the kids while we are all at home together."

I openly talked about it so that others knew that it was something that I was going through, as were many others. I was one of the only people in my peer group that had small kids during this time.

I consistently shared my working hours, which was a boundary I put in place, to meet my value of family. I wasn't balanced in anything, except maybe in the guilt I felt of not meeting the needs of all my roles. I consistently messaged my team, peers, and others in the organization about why my schedule was shifting and why it was important.

It was a very intentional practice, to share that with others. It benefited my team too. By sharing what I was doing, I was giving them permission to do the same thing. At times of uncertainty, consistency in messaging is even more powerful.

Be consistent in your messaging throughout your work and life. You'll start seeing your team repeating or using the same language you use. You'll see them anticipate what's important to you after time. You'll start building a consistency that they didn't even know that they craved in this ever-changing world of work.

You can create consistency for your team by consistently aligning yourself with your values then proactively asserting and clarifying them. In the next section, we'll talk about how using your values consistently will help you create connection.

creating connection

Remember when I almost didn't go to my second workout class because it was too hard? Fast-forward five years: I loved rowing so much that I invested in a Water Rower for our house so I could row whenever I wanted. I love the accessibility of the rower and being able to more easily meet my core value of balance, even if that means not being with my rowing friends in a workout class.

With my Water Rower, and as one does around the new year, I set a huge resolution to challenge myself: I would row one million meters in a year!

On a rowing machine, meters rowed is one of the metrics that is tracked, just as how a treadmill tracks the total distance you've run in a given amount of time. Rowing one million meters in a year sounds huge. It is, but it is very achievable if you have one thing: consistency. By doing some quick math, I realized that I needed around 84,000 meters per month, or 21,000 meters per week, to reach my goal by the end of the year.

In each rowing class, I would average around 5,000 meters. At that time, I was attending a few classes a week and rowing at home too. It was a doable goal if I was consistent every week. Some weeks, I was out of town traveling for work or with family and didn't have access to a rowing machine. But other weeks, I rowed on my Water Rower while watching rowing video workouts, watching Netflix, or listening to music.

Since I had shared my goal with a few friends, when I was in class they checked in with me. They asked how my goal was going. It helped keep me accountable to the goal and to my values of balance and achievement.

By June, I was behind my midpoint goal. After each workout, I would log how many meters I had rowed in an app on my phone. Looking at the number of meters I'd accumulated kept me motivated to keep going. By October I had caught up. I knew I would meet my goal because I'd kept going. The last few months of the year felt like a countdown to meeting my goal.

In the middle of December, I was taking a rowing class and realized that I was close to meeting my goal. At the end of class, instead of stopping, I asked the instructor if I could keep going. I had rowed 8,000 meters and only had 6,000 more to reach my one million meters mark. The instructor and a few other rowing friends kept me company while the meters ticked away.

I lived my core values of balance and achievement and met my goal through consistency in that year. That's what success meant for me in that season. I was able to share that goal with others, showing them what was important for me. And in that final push, they cheered me on as I finished my one million meter goal.

What does living your values mean for you? What does it say about you?

Just like you have your core values that are important to you, the members of your team have core values that are important to them as individuals.

Your values can create connection between you and the individuals on your team and between team members.

In this section of the Values First Framework, we are going deeper into your values journey. Next, you'll learn how to build team connection through values, connect your core values to organizational values, and create team values and behaviors together.

VALUES CAN BE USED TO CREATE CONNECTION AMONG INDIVIDUALS

There are many opportunities for you to create connection with your team, but oftentimes we miss those chances. One common place for team connection is in team off-sites or retreats. I often get asked, "Laura, I'm having a team meeting in a few weeks, and we need to spend some time doing team stuff. We have a few hours; what should we do?"

The "team stuff." The bonding stuff, the fluffy stuff, right? What usually happens is the few hours that they've put aside for the "team stuff" gets deprioritized. They really want to prioritize it, but they don't know what to focus on, and it becomes an afterthought.

I want your "team stuff" to be more than an afterthought and more than a one hour session at an annual off-site for strategic planning. If done right, you'll be setting your strategic plan in a different and more meaningful way. Your team culture will be integrated into how you do strategic planning and how you get the results you want.

TEAM REFLECTION

I've made this easy for you and have created a Building Team Connection Tool Kit that you can incorporate into any team meeting. By using the Values First Framework, you can use values as the connecting point to learn more about the individuals that make up a team. You can find this exercise in the Values First Teams Workbook.

What types of teams should do this exercise? Below are a few instances that would benefit most from the Building Team Connection Tool Kit:

- A new leader joins an existing team
- A new team member joins an existing team

- Two or more teams come together under one leader
- An existing team enters a new fiscal year
- A cross-functional team comes together to accomplish a strategic goal
- A new leadership team is formed
- The board of directors holds an annual planning session
- A new C-suite member joins an existing senior leadership team
- A new employee resource group is formed
- A new committee at a non-profit is formed
- An annual department meeting is held off-site
- A university or educational institution that has never done a team off-site before
- A team is working through conflict
- (Hint: Any team can benefit from this exercise!)

The main components of the exercise are having each team member complete the Values First Worksheet and sharing their values and what those values mean to them.

Then each team member completes the Values Alignment worksheet. This allows the team to reflect on the organization's values and how their core values overlap with the organization's. Here you are identifying your values alignment with the organization.

One leader that I worked with resonated most with their company's value of commitment to community and shared a story with the team of when they personally saw the company's value in action. They saw that, when a hurricane hit their local community, the company donated products to local charities to support community members in need.

Having a team session like this prioritizes connection and intentionality. By prioritizing the team's time, you are modeling that this kind of thing is important to you as a leader. You are showing them what you value. You are learning about what they value. You can then utilize this information to have deeper discussions with the team or with each direct report one-on-one.

These kinds of things don't have to be overcomplicated. This is a simple way to bring people together to share what matters most to them.

The Building Team Connection Tool Kit is the foundation of the next step in creating your Values First Team. Let's see how these simple techniques can make a world of difference in creating a values-led team.

more than words

A favorite song of mine growing up as a pre-teen—when I had more emotions than actual life experience—was "More than Words" by Extreme.[5] The song is about showing how you feel with actions, not just saying empty phrases.

While I now have a fully formed frontal lobe and can process emotions rationally as an adult, I still stand by the sentiment of the song. Words are not enough; I need to see action to back them up.

How many times have you seen words without behaviors to back it up within an organization? I've walked into countless corporate buildings where the company's values are proudly posted on the wall in grandiose lettering. But when you talk to individuals in the organization and ask them how those words look in action, they can't. Employees want and need to see more than words. They need to see the behaviors that back up the words. Seeing their leaders model values with behaviors will boost employee commitment.[6]

What do values look like in practice? How do you know if you are living them? Would someone else know that you were living your values if they were watching from an outside perspective?

In your Values Statement, you broke down the behaviors that link back to your values. Now we'll do the same as we create team values and associated behaviors.

Why do you need team values if you have organizational values and individual values? Is that too many layers of values?

Sometimes organizational values can be vague or too all-encompassing. You may not have the power to change or update corporate-level values. By building out team values, you are prioritizing the company's values to your team's work.

Leaders can impact their organization's culture through their own personality and values. A recent study from researchers at Stanford and Massachusetts Institute of Technology (MIT) hypothesized that a CEO's personality affects their behavior, which in turn shapes the culture of an organization.[7] The leader's personality and values likely cascade into the organization and set the culture: they are linked.

This research suggests that there is no perfect personality for the leadership role of CEO. If that's the case for this leadership position, then this theory may be extrapolated to other leadership positions as well. You get to take your personality and values and bring it into an organization or team to create the culture. To model it. To build it.

You can create cultures that are aligned with what's important to you. It means that you need to pay attention to the things that you model because they can cascade down positively or negatively. Most importantly, since there isn't a perfect personality for leadership, there's room for your personality, your values, and how you lead.

That said, it may be very tempting to build out team values yourself. You may already have how you want it to go and the values you want for your team culture mapped out in your head. You are leading the team after all.

This is one of the most common mistakes I see. You have your Values Statement, your vision of your team, and you know how to get to your strategy. It is so clear to you. It won't be so clear to everyone else.

The last time I looked, you weren't the only one in the team. You are only one person. To lead the team, you need to include them. Most likely, their ideas will be similar or even better than yours. By including them in building out the team's culture, they will have a part in it. They will feel included. Their voices will be heard.[8] Their values will be represented.

You are also enabling them to build something together with you. Most likely they didn't build the company values—your team will give their values a voice.

By building team values, they can have a stake in the team's culture. They can have their fingerprints on it. It is beneficial to you and them to build team values together.

The team should define what the values mean to them and how they engage and demonstrate those values. You are creating the team culture that individuals will thrive in to get the team and organizational results you want—this is through values alignment. Individuals will see alignment between their own values and the organization's and their own values and the team's values. Values alignment at the team and organizational level is a very powerful thing.

Building team values is the next step in the Values First Framework. As a collective exercise, you can lead your team yourself or utilize a facilitator to bring your team through the process. Many leaders I work with decide to participate in the session themselves, as they realize the benefits of a facilitator.

A few benefits:

- You can participate with the team, allowing yourself to be a part of the process, not directing the process
- You'll have more time to ensure you have self-awareness of how you are showing up in the room with your team
- Your team will have an increased sense of "we are in this together"
- You'll have an objective perspective from an outside facilitator

- The facilitator can guide discussion and ensure timeliness of exercises
- The facilitator can raise questions or name a theme or topic that a team member may not be able to
- The facilitator can utilize different techniques to ensure everyone gets their voice heard
- The facilitator can give you coaching on the side when needed

Many leaders opt to work directly with me or a Values First Framework–certified facilitator to build their team values. Sometimes the best person to facilitate the session may be an internal resource, especially one who is a certified Values First facilitator or a human resources facilitator with knowledge of the Values First Framework and approach.

~~bbbb~~ TEAM REFLECTION

Go to your Values First Teams Workbook to review the Team Values Worksheet. There you'll find an example of a completed Team Values and Behaviors Worksheet. Similarly to how you isolate individual core values, your team will work together to prioritize team values that link back to the organization's values.

THE ANATOMY OF A BEHAVIOR

If we only talk about team values at a high level, they will only be words on walls. We want to describe values at the behavioral level. Some teams like to have values that are a descriptive phrase. For instance, instead of a value simply named "collaboration," they may title it "collaboration with heart" or "purposeful collaboration."

After naming their team values, teams can describe the behaviors associated with that value. I was facilitating a team values session for two teams that would be combined and report to one leader. The teams weren't new, but the team structure was. The leader prioritized this session to build team connection and to align on how individuals would be working together as a new team. In the session, the team prioritized a value of "focus on balance." The next step was to build out behaviors.

I asked them, "What does this value look like in action? How will you know when you see someone doing it, living it?"

The team wrote out a list of behaviors associated with focus on balance and how they would be able to see the value in their everyday work together. Some behaviors were for them as individuals; other behaviors focused on how they would interact with one another.

I asked one team member to elaborate on the behavior she had written down. "Tell me more about honoring out of office. What do you mean by that?"

"When I'm out of the office on paid time off, I need to honor it for myself. I need to not check my email, not call into the meeting. And as a team member, if someone is out of the office, then know that and don't bug them. We could do a better job at preparing to be gone and communicating our schedules of when we are out."

The team went on to discuss other behaviors and prioritized five behaviors that encompassed their team value of focus on balance.

Value: Focus on balance
Behaviors:
- Intentionally, frequently check in with each other
- Ask for help when you need it
- Assess trade-offs, communicate realistic deadlines
- Calibrate priorities weekly
- Honor the out of office

The core value of focus on balance was important for this team, as they would be rolling out multiple company-wide initiatives. They knew that if they didn't focus on balance ruthlessly, then they would likely burn themselves out. The leader of this group was very aligned with the team in prioritizing this value as one of their core values.

That's not always the case. What happens if the leader of the team has a different perspective on core values for the team?

In your role, people are watching you: they see what you do and don't do, how you react and what you react to, and what is urgent and what isn't. The fact that you are interested in doing this work means that you are a great leader. If you weren't, you wouldn't be spending time building your team culture. You'd only be interested in results.

As all eyes are often on you, self-awareness is key. In this work, you are still the leader even as you build this culture with your team.

Here are some mistakes to avoid as the leader in the room during the team session.

- Talking too much
- Not listening to all ideas
- Overriding the consensus in the room
- Not being present (physically there, but not paying attention)

I had a client who was in his leadership role at a non-profit for over five years, and we partnered together to codify the culture of his department of over forty people. The organization had a vision and a mission that the team anchored their goals to, but they wanted to build out their team values to continue to inspire and motivate everyone.

We partnered to build out their team values in an in-person workshop at their annual department off-site. In advance, I worked with the leader and the leadership team. On the day of the workshop, everything was going to plan.

We started with the individual values exercise, which brought up insights regarding the lack of work-life balance in the organization. One of the themes I have seen commonly with non-profits, support professions, and human resources organizations is that individuals who gravitate to these industries value doing things for others. Their individual values are often others-centered: impact, community, sustainability, serving others, and caring for others. Often when they reflect on their own values, they don't have a core value that only serves themselves.

That was also the case here: each of these non-profit leaders was over-indexed on core values serving others. Don't get me wrong, that's what makes them great at their jobs and the reason why they have had careers in non-profit work. But this has come up so often in this work that now I challenge leaders to do another review of their values.

"I need you to have at least one value that is just for you. Sometimes that looks like balance, freedom, or health. What is yours? If you don't have at least one of your values that is just for you, I need you to add one to your list. What will you call it?"

If you don't have an individual value for caring for yourself when you are in the career of serving others, then you are more likely to burn out. I want you to have a sustainable career, and doing something for you is going to be important.

At the meeting, individuals started to add a value to their core values based on that discussion, and then we went on to build out team values. We broke out into separate rooms and came back together to debrief team values. As groups started presenting their ideas on team values, I noticed a theme emerging. Every group had a value of prioritizing wellness listed as one of their proposed team values.

I wondered who would be the first to notice this, or the first to highlight it. It wasn't the department leader, but one of the leaders of the leadership team who said, "It is so interesting that every group mentioned wellness for our team as a priority. Before today,

I would never have guessed that that would have been a theme of our work." Many other colleagues gave approving nods in agreement. However, the department leader looked visibly concerned when his direct report brought this theme up.

It was about time for a break, so I stopped the group and brought the leader aside.

"How do you think the session is going?" I asked.

"I think it is good but feel like sometimes they use these kinds of meetings to complain about work-life balance. The comment about prioritizing wellness, we should always be doing that. Isn't that inferred for what we do? I don't think it needs to be part of our team values," he stated quickly.

"We should always be doing it, but are we?" I asked.

"Well, I try to. I mean, I do it personally, but isn't that up to each person? Why would it need to be part of team values?"

"Wellness is an important team value to consider, especially since each small group came up with it separately. When your small group talked about it, what kinds of things were brought up?"

"They talked mostly about prioritization, peak hours, and how often people aren't taking their vacation days."

"Do you think that's accurate for the department?"

"Generally, yes. But we've been making some progress on it."

"Here's my observation. Multiple groups came up with it, so it feels like something we should pay attention to. Highlighting it as a team value means that you'll be able to continue to make focused progress toward it. Leaving it out will be a clear signal to the team that prioritizing wellness isn't important."

"Yeah, the group is right. We need to prioritize it. I guess my initial reaction was more about my feelings about not making as much progress as I'd like. By including it, we are giving it the focus it deserves."

This leader was open to getting feedback in the moment on

how he could show up differently in this session. If he didn't listen to the team's feedback, he may have overridden the consensus in the room. That could have felt very demotivating to team members.

As you build your team values, make sure that you pay attention to how you are feeling in the moment. How are you showing up, and how is that going to impact the room and the outcomes?

As you review the team values, take a lesson from this team. How are you caring for yourselves? Review your team values and ensure that you have at least one value that focuses on team health, balance, or sustainability. You need it for yourself individually, and you need it for the team too.

There are multiple ways to get to a team's five to seven values and behaviors. You can do an in-person session, or you can do a series of virtual sessions broken out over time. The important part is that you prioritize the team's culture and that you do it together.

By building team values together, you are identifying what matters most to you all and creating connection.[9] You are defining what success means by living those values together, in the same boat, all rowing in the same direction. **You are living out values together, in connection.**

The synchronicity of building values together makes a team able and willing to show up for each other. Whether you are in a gym or a board room, you're aligned as an individual, an organization, and a team all rowing in sync. That synchronicity gives you confidence as an individual and as a team.

Now that you're in sync, let's help you stay that way with regular values audits.

audit time

Audit how your team is currently living up to the team's values and behaviors. Review your time, energy, systems, and the processes your team uses to ensure alignment with the team's values.

Values First Team Workbook Tools in this section:

- Team Values Check-In
- Values First Meetings Worksheet
- Team Systems and Processes Audit

stay tuned in

After meeting my one million meters in a year goal, I felt accomplished personally. This gave me professional confidence starting in a new C-suite role. My work travel increased, and I got to visit bucket list places like Australia and South Africa within the first few months. During the last day of the South Africa trip at a team dinner, I started feeling intense pain in my ribs and back.

I was miserable and had to lie down on the concrete as we waited for the Uber to bring us back to our hotel. I wasn't sure what I had done to my back, but it wasn't good. I had less than twenty-four hours until I was supposed to get on a twenty-plus-hour flight back home.

The next day I got medical treatment and was cleared for the long flight home. I had had chronic back pain many years prior due to a car accident, but this pain felt different. Eventually I was prescribed physical therapy. During my recovery, I didn't row for months. My goal was to increase my mobility and strength and decrease my pain.

Up until then, I was in the best shape I'd been in my life. During recovery, I felt frustrated, mad, and impatient that relief was taking so long. After many months of physical therapy, my progress plateaued, and I considered surgery for the first time. But I wouldn't do it before I squeezed in that last international work trip to Panama.

While I couldn't meet my value of balance, I had started

over-indexing on other things, like my value of achievement. This meant working more. I had to reevaluate what was most important to me and after some counsel from a few close friends, decided to schedule back surgery and take several weeks off to heal.

The pain relief from back surgery wasn't immediate but did come over time. I used that time to reevaluate what success looked like for me. Progress meant being able to take short walks outside and extending the distance week after week. My pain decreased substantially over time as well. And eventually I got cleared to row again.

Audits give us a time to assess, adjust, and reevaluate our goals and versions of success for each season of life. Sometimes the time to reassess is clear to us, with our bodies screaming at us in pain. Other times we don't have the clarity to see it for ourselves and need the help of others to clue us in.

I was facilitating a section of a team meeting for a leader and his direct reports. The leader, the chief operating officer (COO), kicked off the meeting. I listened and then watched the reactions of his direct reports in the room. They were mostly engaged, and some were taking notes. After some time, many started looking at their watches and phones. The COO was known to be long winded: he had lots of thoughts and seemed to think through them aloud.

Throughout the morning, I noticed the leader—a longtime direct report of the COO—next to me looking at his smartwatch. Specifically, he was looking at the timer on the watch. He was timing something. Was he timing something for medication? Or something he needed to remember? He kept checking the watch.

Then I realized. He was timing how long the COO was talking without interruption. The current timer on his watch read over fourteen minutes. He was timing the duration and frequency of when his leader was going on and on and on about something.

Fourteen minutes of talking meant no questions. Fourteen

minutes of no pauses, no listening, no self-awareness. Fourteen minutes of no engagement.

His direct reports had disengaged because the leader was clear that the only voice in the room he wanted to hear was his own. That leader wasn't tuned in.

How can you and your team stay tuned in? By grounding yourselves back into your team values.

In this section of the Values First Framework, we are going to Audit Time. We'll check in to see how the team is doing on the team values you built together. You'll audit how the team spends their time and how the team values do and do not show up as you work together. As a team, which behaviors are your strengths and which are your gaps?

The Team Values Check-In is an audit of the team on the values right now. Our values aren't aspirational. It isn't a dream goal to get to all of them. The behaviors should be attainable, even if you may not be great at all of them yet. Most likely, there will be some that your team are better at than others.

INDIVIDUAL REFLECTION

Go to your Values First Team Workbook to review the Team Values Check-In, which has two parts.

- Assessing yourself against the team values and behaviors
- Assessing the team against the team values and behaviors

You'll start your assessment by reviewing your own behavior. You'll review three questions for each team value:

- How consistently am I living the team value (doing the behaviors)?
- How do I feel about it?
- Are your individual values aligned with the team's values?

Be honest here. Maybe you are great at collaborating but not as good at modeling taking time off from work for your team. How do you feel about it? Have each member of the team do this as well. What are they individually doing well at, and what isn't a strength?

You may be consistently over-indexing on a few of the behaviors but neglecting others. You don't have to perfectly show up, and you shouldn't. That's not attainable. You need to not only believe in the values, but also do them. The "do what I say, not as I do" leadership style isn't a great one. If your team doesn't see you doing the behaviors, then they won't think they can do them themselves. The team values just become those words on walls and not something your team truly believes.

To maintain the consistency of your values, it is important to check in on them. In Values First, I suggest you check in with your own core values every ninety days. My recommendation for checking in on Team Values is the same: check in on your team values as a team every ninety days.

~~kkkk~~ TEAM REFLECTION

Next, you'll assess how the team is living the team values. Have a conversation about each of the team values with a team member. For each team value, answer the following questions:

- Is the team living the team values and behaviors?
- What is a positive experience associated with the team values?
- What team values and behaviors are not done as consistently?
- What team values can you celebrate?
- What team values do you need to recalibrate?

Reviewing how the team is living the team values is not a place for aspiration. The team values you created aren't long-term plans for how you want the team to work together. They should be attainable now: real behaviors.

After doing their Team Check-In reflection, one team I worked with identified their team value of innovation as their biggest gap. It was still very important to their long-term success but, given their workload, they wondered if it was too aspirational.

Would they really be able to live out this core value?

Their workloads were too heavy, and they weren't prioritizing innovation. They discussed that their demanding priorities kept shifting, creating new things to respond to and getting in the way. They were in reactive mode. During reactive mode, innovation isn't easy to accomplish. This was part of their organizational culture, and they knew that they wouldn't be able to stop this from happening.

The disparity between the reactivity of the organizational culture and their team value of innovation was causing tension, a sign of values misalignment. The team needed to recalibrate and practice innovation intentionally, or it would stay solely aspirational.

In the next section you'll assess the processes that are key indicators of intentionality when working as a team: meetings, systems, technology, and communication. By understanding your key indicators, you can make sure your team values don't stay solely aspirational.

this could have been an email

More than eleven million meetings are held every day in the United States.[10] Sometimes I feel like I've been invited to attend at least a million of those. Ready for another unsurprising and underwhelming statistic? Only 30 percent of those meetings are considered productive. Yep, that feels about right. We have too many meetings, and we aren't great at them.

Living your team's values isn't just about the collective behavior of the individuals in the team. It is about how you spend time together. It is about what you do in that time.

How do you spend time as a team? The most common answer that comes up when I ask this to teams is overwhelmingly *meetings*.

Meetings can have their own culture in an organization. What are your team meetings like?

One team that I worked with talked about how they met weekly as a team and often went around the room (or Zoom) with the updates from the week. They spent most of their time updating their manager, the department leader, on their progress toward their goals and things that were keeping them from their goals. This is a very common team meeting culture: the "update meeting culture." This is a form of team communication. The benefit is that it centralizes messaging. People get to know what everyone is doing. The leader is kept in the loop. Often issues are raised, which escalates problems to the leader and peer group.

What are the drawbacks to "update meeting culture"? Here are a few:

- The meetings become a laundry list of tasks
- Each individual talks about and is focused on their own tasks and communicating those
- Conversations are very surface level
- They are not strategic
- Problem-solving doesn't happen

Have you been a part of a team that has an "update meeting culture"? How did those meetings feel? Not that productive, right? This type of meeting culture has a feeling of "this meeting could have been an email." How did you feel about the leader of that team? Were they viewed as strategic? Did they know how to get the best from the team? Most likely no.

As you audit your team, how would you describe the team's current meeting culture? Is it productive? Do you meet often enough? Too often?

Let me ask you this more important question:

What is the meeting culture that will align with the team's values?

TEAM REFLECTION

Go to the Values First Teams Workbook to fill out the Values First Meetings Worksheet. You'll review and fill this out as a team.

- What values are most important to live in our team meetings?
- How often should we meet? Duration?
- What activities should we prioritize, and are they

aligned with our values?
- How often should we have one-on-ones to complement our team meeting cadence?
- What other systems of communication should we use to augment our team meetings?
  - Agendas: Standing agendas with dynamic content
  - Facilitators: Who is leading which topic?
  - Notetakers: Who is documenting what happened? Take turns with this, as all too often women take the lead on taking notes as an administrative job. This is everyone's job regardless of how great their handwriting is.
  - Prework: Being prepared with prework in advance as the facilitator and doing the readings in advance as a prepared team member.

On my podcast, *You Belong in the C-Suite*, I interviewed Yari Ising, a productivity expert.[11] She shares her expertise in building better meetings for her and her teams and increasing efficiency by using the essentialist mindset of being ruthless with her time.

She described that, as teams, we hold onto our rituals and standards of operation. Often, we don't audit the effectiveness of our meetings. We don't often review what is serving us.

Everyone wants fewer meetings. And everyone wants better meetings.

Yari's team conducts quarterly after-action reviews. She asks her team questions like:

- What are we doing well?
- What can be improved?
- What do you want to see more of?
- What do you want to see less of?

- What other thoughts do you want to share?

Her team shares their responses through a confidential survey in advance of their quarterly meeting.

In one of those meetings, a team member wanted to repurpose a brainstorming meeting that they already had on the calendar. They suggested to use it for culture-building purposes instead. Instead of adding another meeting on their calendars, they repurposed a timeslot that already existed.

Let's get back to the team that was feeling tension between their reactive organizational culture and their team value of innovation. They needed to recalibrate what innovation looked like for them. What would it look like for them to practice innovation consistently?

They discussed having dedicated working sessions to solve more long-term problems. That would require them to do something differently. The team decided to build in intentional working sessions in their leadership team meetings held every other month. In their monthly meeting, they'd prioritize making time to solve a specific long-term problem that would impact the team.

Living a team value and the behaviors that support it is just that: intentional. If you aren't practicing the value currently, what can you do to prioritize it differently? It doesn't have to be a huge shift in behavior—instead it can be an intentional way to shift the time spent together to focus on that behavior.

How can you repurpose an existing meeting to accomplish another goal that aligns with your team values? What changes do you need to make to get the meeting culture you want?

SYSTEMS, TECHNOLOGY, AND COMMUNICATION

Meetings are a big part of how you spend time and make decisions with your team. But meetings aren't the only ways you communicate with your team and with others internally and externally. What systems, technologies, and communication methods work to uphold the team's values? Which ones detract from living the team's values?

The next review I want you to do isn't super glamorous, but it may save you a precious commodity: time. I want you to audit the systems, technologies, and processes you use to communicate internally and externally. Systems can include software like a customer relationship management (CRM) system. It can also mean the day-to-day communication systems like email, Slack, and Microsoft Office Suite. Many teams and organizations use PowerPoint to communicate, spending hours upon hours creating slide decks on what business decisions to make or why one idea is better than another and sharing them with each other.

༺༺༺༺ TEAM REFLECTION

Go to your Values First Teams Workbook and complete the Team Systems and Process Audit. Write down all the systems you use to communicate with each other.

Example:

METHOD	USE
PowerPoint	Document meeting agendas, socialize project plans
Smartsheet	Project management
Slack	Informal communication on various channels, show availability
Weekly update report	Weekly project updates
Monthly client report	Monthly client outcomes
Email	Requests, messaging to inform

Next, answer the following questions for each of the systems or technology methods listed:

- Does this system align with our team values? How?
- Is its use detracting from our team values? In what way?

After completing the Team Systems and Process Audit, one team noted that their use of Slack reflected their collaboration on dedicated channels for projects. However, they also noted that they overused it to get ahold of team members, often in the evening hours. This felt like a big detractor of their team value of sustainability. If they were always available to answer a question, even in the name of a team value of collaboration, then wasn't that a disservice to the team value of sustainability? The short answer was, yes. They were sacrificing one value for another.

This highlighted the team's overuse of a technology without guidelines or boundaries. The team knew that they needed better guidelines to really live their values. They knew that, to really be intentional, setting a boundary around technology was a right next step.

Sometimes you need to be more rigid, sometimes more flexible. Audits help you make sure that your values stay aligned while your goals and your definition of success shift, all so you can keep up with the ever-changing landscape of life and business.

Next, we'll incorporate accountabilities to ensure we support individuals and the team. I'll show you how to do this by setting strong values-based boundaries and systems to support those boundaries.

life boundaries

Establish boundaries for the life of your team to show care for team values and set the priorities and accountabilities you need.

Values First Teams Workbook tools in this section:

- Build a Boundary Worksheet
- Team Boundary Worksheet

building and keeping boundaries

One of my favorite icebreaker questions is, "What's one thing you've wanted to do but haven't yet?" I got to answer this question in a team meeting at the beginning of my first role in the C-suite. I was finishing my New Year's resolution of rowing one million meters on my indoor rowing machine. That goal was all about consistency, racking up the meters with each workout.

But that's not how I answered the question. My answer to this question was something I'd been thinking about for a while. I wanted to try rowing on the water. This was in 2018, and in that year, I traveled so often my chronic back pain flared up, and I ended up in physical therapy and eventually back surgery. I didn't get on the water that year or the year after.

After recovering from surgery, I did get back on my indoor rower, which was a big milestone for me. In the back of my mind, I still thought about what it would be like out on the water. But I didn't take any action on it. When I look back now, I feel like I wasn't living my values by staying within my comfort zone. I thought I was living my value of balance, but I was ignoring my value of growth. I had unintentionally set a boundary to keep me safe.

In this chapter I'm going to show you the common mistakes around boundaries and help you look at your boundaries holistically as a system. We will use the Values First Framework in the Life Boundaries section, first starting with your individual boundaries. Then we'll build team boundaries linked to your team values.

COMMON MISTAKES IN BUILDING BOUNDARIES

You have the power to model boundaries for the team, but you can also model burnout. Can you guess which one most people see from their managers?

I wish I could tell you it was modeling boundaries, but alas, it is the modeling of burnout behavior. Always being accessible, checking email at all hours of the night, being the first to respond to email in the morning, and not regularly taking vacation are all behaviors I see often.

When working with leaders on their values for the last several years, I've been grateful to hear from different readers and podcast listeners about their values. Burnout has come up in those conversations and in the conversations with my coaching clients. As leaders are identifying their core values, more and more often also realize they need to add a value that prioritizes themselves and use their boundaries to reduce and prevent burnout.

Values of self-care, balance, sustainability, and being centered show up on their lists of core values.

Unsurprisingly, these values are often accompanied by feelings of misalignment, unhappiness, and anxiety. They are areas of life that are important but aren't getting prioritized within the schedules of busy executives.

These values are also the ones that people aren't generally living. They are winning on other values, but these values, not so much.

Now, people are adding or redefining these values for themselves. When I ask the leaders that I coach, why are these ones falling through the gap? When I inquire about what's holding them back from holding space for living these values, they say, "work priorities."

It's hard to show up for your team, for your boss, meet your goals, and show up for your family. It isn't uncommon to be double or triple booked, to survive on the fumes of your morning coffee, look up and realize it is two in the afternoon.

You are leaning into all of it. Just like we were told to do: lean on in.

When does that leave time for you?

I've leaned in too far to be everything for everyone at work more than once. I do it because I'm driven partly by achievement—that's one of my values. Overworking used to be the default: it was an overuse of that value. Those days I was exhausted. I was easily frustrated. I would ruminate over different things I had or had not said in meetings.

After working on building more boundaries that were tied to my other values—of family, of balance—things started to shift. My mindset started to shift. The way I spent my time started to shift.

Over time, I learned that I need to practice and prioritize the value of balance to a greater degree. For me, balance doesn't mean work-life balance. That's not a thing. It means building a boundary that I prioritize.

Instead, balance is feeling centered and feeling like I am in control of my time and my day. I need to overuse that value because that hasn't previously been the default. I'm still trying to unlearn *years* of overusing my achievement value. I'm trying to get my value of balance to be the default.

And what that means for me is to hold space for my boundaries, which are specifically aligned with my value of balance. Preserving that time for me. Holding that space for me.

It is hard to do, let me tell you.

I hear from a variety of leaders that they used to have a great exercise routine that they did consistently. They used to have a hobby, they used to love to cook, they used to <fill in the blank>.

They've stopped doing that thing they used to because things have gotten really busy at work.

If you used to do something, that means that at some point you prioritized it. It was fun. It brought you joy, stress relief, happiness, or creativity.

And then the default took over: work . . .

I want to get you back to that place, where you are putting that thing back into your life. You should hold that boundary for yourself, and that should be your default.

What will happen when people see their senior leaders do that? It is going to show them that it is okay for them to do it too. It will give them permission to do the same.

I want that for you, and I want that for your team.

Do you know who is great at setting boundaries? Younger generations like Gen Z are known for consistently setting boundaries. They want managers who are good at that too.[12]

Let's refresh your memory on how you can do this. Within the Values First Framework, there's a three-step method to build a boundary.

1. **Tie it to a value.** When you couple a boundary with a value, you are creating intrinsic motivation. Intrinsic motivators drive behavior change by tapping into internal feelings that are fulfilling.[13] In this case, we are tying boundaries to a core value that is very important to us. By doing that, we are more likely to keep the boundary.
2. **Set up a system.** Whether that is through technology, an accountability partner, investment of money or time, or something else, build a system that works for you to enable the boundary.

3. **Celebrate consistency.** We don't celebrate enough. Remember, we don't usually have time to. We run to the next thing. The boundary that you build and keep will inherently be fulfilling when you do it. But I want you to celebrate with some positive reinforcement to help you.

Recently a reader reached out to me and said, "The boundaries exercises were *really* eye opening. The concept of celebrating consistency was pretty mind blowing—I think, in reality, it can feel really hard to celebrate setting a boundary because it often feels like you're disappointing someone. The concept of intentionally celebrating boundary setting was such a powerful thing to hear from someone else."

Yes, you may be celebrating disappointing someone. But guess what? You are not disappointing yourself. Celebrate that, celebrate not letting yourself down. Celebrate that you kept your boundary intact and then do it again.

I know this step is hard. Unlearning is hard. Saying no is hard. Building a new habit is hard. Almost always, like clockwork, near the end of a rowing workout when exhaustion sets in, I feel my legs burning, and my rowing form starts to fall apart, my rowing coach will say, "This set is hard, but the regret of not finishing is harder."

You already know what disappointing yourself feels like. So instead of feeling that again, celebrate the hard work you put in by keeping your boundary.

Here's what not prioritizing yourself looks like for my clients:

- Five minutes before our meeting, they send me a quick one-line email: "Need to reschedule"
- "I'll be there soon, jumping from one call to another and haven't had a chance to grab lunch . . . "
- "I completely messed up my calendar and double-booked my time; can we reschedule?"

On the other end of the spectrum, I hear:

- "I'm so thankful that I'm meeting with you today because I need a breather—things have been so hectic."
- "Our meeting is perfectly timed because I have something I want to run by you."
- "Oh my goodness, I didn't realize how much I needed this time to take a step back and reflect. I always leave our time together energized."

We are overscheduling our lives. Let me rephrase that: we are prioritizing our work. We've been programmed to. That is the norm, especially in America.[14] We are extending our days into the evenings. You may be doing this because you are doing multiple roles simultaneously: your company may have had layoffs, or maybe you got promoted and you are doing your new job and your old job.

I want to give you the permission to do one thing that you need for yourself. I want you to answer the question "What do I need more of right now?"

I could have also asked you "What do you need less of?" but I didn't ask you that on purpose. I think that reframing is very important. You are giving something to yourself. I'm asking you what can you do for yourself, that you need more of—that you can control. That you can act on.

What do you need more of right now? Is it a boundary?

Do you need more time? Do you need more sleep? Do you need more peace? Do you need more help? Do you need more support? Do you need your workout or even a walk outside?

There are always going to be more things to do than time to do them. The bigger your role, the higher the leadership position, the more things coming at you. To sustain your impact, you need to set your pace. It sounds counterintuitive, but I am going to ask you to work less. I'm going to ask you to prioritize something that you need right now.

Right now your life may feel frenetic. Like your only choice is to be reactive. You have so much on your plate. You don't want to let anyone down.

I'm giving you permission to do the thing that you need for yourself. I really want you to give yourself that permission, but if that isn't going to work then just say, "Laura said I need to." I'm urging you to.

INDIVIDUAL REFLECTION

Go to your Values First Teams Workbook to complete the Boundary Builder Worksheet. What boundary do you need most right now in order to live your values? Model that consistently for your team.

For one leader, having established values and boundaries not only helped her transition successfully to a C-suite role but also influenced her team and company.

boundaries in transition

Mikayla, a finance leader, joined my You Belong in the C-Suite group coaching cohort as she transitioned into her new C-suite role. She was in this new role without ever having aspirations for it. Is it something that she really wanted? She was hesitant because she knew what the demands would be. Or she thought she did.

She took the role under a few conditions: that her flexible schedule would remain as-is to meet the needs of her family with young kids; that she would keep her office close to her team instead of moving over with her peers in the C-suite; and that she would get support through an external coaching program. She went in with these conditions as non-negotiables, already building boundaries before even taking the job!

Mikayla identified her core values as family, development, respect, self-care, and accountability. As she settled into her role, she realized how important the boundaries that she'd started with were, but also knew she needed more boundaries. She started building boundaries around quiet time for herself on Saturday mornings with a solo walk on the beach.

She started utilizing her values as an anchor of her leadership style. As head of finance and one of the only women in the C-suite, she knew that her value of accountability was paramount.

She started asking more questions tied to accountability. How were they as a finance team and those within her peer group holding each other to their commitments?

Her team built a dashboard to track organizational metrics that could be viewed by leadership and the company. They utilized a stoplight assessment (red, yellow, green) to hold each other accountable. C-suite discussions centered around issues that were assigned as yellow or red, and green results were celebrated.

Being the person to stand up for the team's values can feel lonely sometimes. When the C-suite started to hold each other accountable, it was hard. Utilizing the stoplight assessment was an exercise of auditing in real time. They took deep looks at their targets. Was it that their targets were wrong or that the team had exercised poor decision-making?

At one point, one of these difficult discussions shook a leader, a peer of Mikayla's. It highlighted his reluctance to align with the company's goals. He wasn't following through on agreements he had made to company targets. After a trend of this behavior, it was clear that his values weren't aligned with the organization's. He soon left the organization for another opportunity. Even though he was a trusted colleague, Mikayla saw her peer leaving as a sign that his values were in misalignment, which wasn't good for him or the company in the short or long term.

Mikayla now dives into hard conversations with confidence, knowing what her values and boundaries are. She knows that if she detects misalignment with her or the company's values, then the conversation is one she needs to prioritize. She's respected for these conversations. Her peers know where they stand with each other.

Mikayla's leadership has permeated throughout her team to her peers and the overall organization. She now hears the CEO talk about the importance of accountability. The influence that she's had with her values is big. Your influence can be too, especially when you are living in alignment with your values.

As she transitioned into her new role, Mikayla is a great example of how powerful boundaries can be. A year into her new role, Mikayla welcomed a vendor into the office for their annual planning session. The vendor hadn't been on-site since the previous year. She mentioned that the energy felt different in the building—in a good way. Mikayla's values had influenced her team, her peers, and the organization, but most of all her boundaries had protected herself and her family.

One of the most rewarding types of coaching that I do is coaching leaders in transition. Transition may look like multiple things. It could be a leader figuring out their next career move within their company, or it could include transitioning from one company to another company or industry. A transition, by definition, necessitates going *from* one situation and going *to* a new one. You can get pulled back to the old one and dragged into the new one. And in the middle, there is a weird in-between space.

There are three common mistakes I see leaders transitioning in their careers make when it comes to boundaries.

1. Not setting boundaries in the interview process or negotiation with the new organization. That may look like bending over backwards for the new employer and being available at any time for an interview. In one instance, a client mentioned that a prospective employer asked for a work product as a case study. This ended up being unpaid work the client did for the company that the company ultimately used even though the client didn't get the role. If we are bending over backwards in the interview process, this is a sign of what's to come with that employer. Pay attention and have boundaries about what you will or will not do.

The negotiation process with a new employer is another place where leaders often neglect setting boundaries. Leaders go in with certain things they want to negotiate but haven't done the work to establish certain non-negotiables. They aren't negotiating much or at all with the new employer because they don't want to seem ungrateful. Not thinking through non-negotiables is another signal of not having boundaries or caring for what you want or need.

2. Not having boundaries when leaving an organization. This may look like leaders overextending themselves as they are leaving an organization. That could look like giving more time or staying on longer to complete a deliverable, saying they will be available after they leave the organization for questions, or doing work after they have stopped getting paid for that work. I've seen leaders do this: their last day was Friday, and they hop on a call the following week. That's a sign to me that you've not managed your exit of an organization with boundaries. Often you are doing this because you deeply care about your team or organization. And I get that, but that isn't doing you any favors.

3. Not taking a break in between jobs. Some people leave a job on Friday and start again on Monday. If you can afford to take a break, take it. You will need more time than you think.

More often, I see leaders starting their jobs before their first day. They haven't gotten paid yet, and they are starting to get on calls. I get wanting to start the job and get ahead, but this is another thing you can decide not to do.

In my own career transition from one company to another, the interview process had gone on for a while, and they wanted me to travel to a company meeting, all while I was still working at another company. That isn't a thing anyone should be doing. After talking about it, my new employer and I thought, "That's not a good idea." I needed to finish strong at my current employer, take a break, and then transition to the new one. I would miss that "important meeting," but there were other ways that we would ensure my successful transition.

A transition is also the perfect time to start the boundaries you always wanted in your old role that you never had. Start building boundaries in the break before you start your new role. In your old role, do you wish you had a consistent morning routine where you worked out? Start doing that now, so when you start your new role, that's a boundary you are bringing with you.

One thing I did when I started the new role is that I didn't have my work email on my personal phone. I received a work phone, so I had two cell phones: one that I used for work and one for personal use. That allowed me to avoid bringing my work phone with me when I was with my family or at a non-work event. That was a boundary that I intentionally set in my break before I went into my new role. A new employer doesn't know what you did before . . . come in with the boundaries that you want. What do you want in the new role? Make that happen and start it in the space in between jobs.

By not establishing boundaries in the transition, leaders aren't caring for their values and what's important to them. They are instead honoring the values of their previous or future employer. So instead, I want you to establish boundaries for you. Add boundaries in the places where you need them the most in between jobs. Make sure you finish strong at your old organization, figure out what you need in between roles, and bring your boundaries with you into the interviews, negotiations, and your start date at the new company. Build boundaries in all these places. You deserve support in your career transition.

Whether you are in a career transition or not, you need boundaries. Here's a list of small boundaries that can make a large impact.

- Working late catching up on email? Schedule your email to go out the next morning. (I do this using Outlook's Schedule Send feature, and you can do it in Gmail too.)
- Need to prioritize strategy work? Schedule deep thinking time, then put your phone in airplane mode and turn your computer Wi-Fi off during that timeslot to get focused working time.
- Putting off tasks? Pay attention to when you have the most energy during the day. Complete more complex things when you have the most energy.
- Trying to end your workday consistently? Commit to something that is timebound, like a workout class, so you leave when you want. When you must be somewhere at a specific time, it can help you hold yourself accountable.

You will consistently set yourself up for success by building your boundaries over time and making small decisions aligned with your values. Your behavior sets the tone for the team. Once you've set your own boundaries and modeled them for your team, you can focus on building the collective team boundary muscle.

team boundaries

"Boundaries" feels like a loaded term. It is often associated with rules, hard and fast lines, and a winner and a loser. Instead, I want you to reframe it. Boundaries can honor the decision your team has made to lead a values-based life, both professionally and personally. By building boundaries, you are caring for your core values, your team goals, and your individual needs.

Building a boundary for the team consists of the same three steps:

1. **Tie it to a value.** This sets up the importance and the reason behind the boundary for everyone.
2. **Set up a system.** Build a system that the team can use to ensure you live this boundary as a team. This may include a software, a technology, or a new process. What will enable you to live the behaviors that make up that team value and set your team up for success?
3. **Celebrate consistency.** Use positive reinforcement to celebrate when the boundary is used. Call it out, hold space for it, and celebrate it when you see it in action in your life and in the team.

Let's look at how one team built team boundaries to center their team values. A team at a software company prioritized a team value of empowered planning. Here's how they built a boundary tied to their value using the Values First Framework three-step method.

1. **Tie it to a value.** They picked empowered planning, one of their team values that included the following behaviors:
   a. Work ahead to plan from peace, not urgency
   b. Ownership of my area of expertise with a partnership mindset
   c. Bring ideas to make something better
   d. Document so the team can learn and repeat
   e. Grow my expertise as the business grows
2. **Set up a system.** The team targeted communication regarding project questions and process improvement suggestions. They utilized a system of Microsoft Teams channels to leave each other asynchronous messages (instead of emails) during core business hours. If it was outside of business hours, they held it until the following day.
3. **Celebrate consistency.** In each team meeting, a manager highlighted a person on the team that showcased one of the behaviors of empowered planning.

~~bbbb~~ TEAM REFLECTION

Now it is your turn. Go to your Values First Teams Workbook to the Team Boundary Worksheet to build a boundary tied to your team values.

Here are some examples of team boundaries from teams who have already prioritized this work:

- No meeting on Fridays
- Take wellness days
- Plan out all vacation days so nothing is left on the table
- Meetings are during core business hours of 10 a.m.–3 p.m.
- No responding to emails after 7 p.m.

- No attending meetings when on vacation
- Use email prompts when an email is urgent marked as urgent in subject line
- Respond to emails within forty-eight hours
- Give feedback directly to the person, don't triangulate with another person
- No side conversations during meetings
- Don't schedule a meeting unless there is an agenda with clear outcomes

You may need to build multiple boundaries for each team value. As you build these boundaries for your team, you are caring for your team culture. You are caring for the team as a unit. You are caring for each of the individuals in that team. You are creating expectations on how you'll work together. You are saying, "This is how we treat each other. This is what we do, and this is what we don't do."

Additional points to consider in reflection of team boundaries:

- Are there team values that need more boundaries than others?
- Is there a team value that you need to pay more attention to right now?
- What is your individual commitment to team boundaries?
- What happens if you see others not living your values and boundaries?

You've now set your team up for success for building boundaries. Now we are going to double down on celebrating success to reinforce the team culture that will get you the results you want.

As a leader, it can be fulfilling and empowering to enforce value-based boundaries. In a coaching meeting with one client, she mentioned that she was getting ready to go on vacation and was going to not bring her laptop with her. One of the team boundaries they had recently built was to not respond to emails while on vacation. In the past, even if she didn't use her laptop during vacation, she felt better knowing it was with her just in case she needed to log on and address an issue. This time, she wasn't going to bring it. She told her team to text her in case of emergency, and of course they never did. When she got back, she posted about her boundary success—of not bringing her laptop on vacation—in their team Slack channel. By being transparent with her boundary, she increased trust with her team, empowering them and trusting them to lead their work in her absence.

Sometimes you need a boundary urgently to help you through a transition or to mitigate burnout. Other times, you know you need a boundary, but you find a way to ignore it because there isn't a huge sense of urgency around it. It was years before I pursued a boundary tied to my core value of growth.

But one question from Amanda Knox finally got me out of my head to set the boundary and take some action. I'll tell you that story in the next chapter, along with how to double down on celebrating team success to reinforce the team culture that will get you the results you want.

uplifting others

Build the support your team needs to live their values, including modeling behaviors and incorporating rewards and recognition.

Values First Teams Workbook tools in this section:

- Catch Crew Action Worksheet
- Five Questions Worksheet
- CARE Feedback Worksheet
- Team Rewards and Recognition Worksheet
- Team Development Budget Checklist

row, row, row your boat

I'm so used to being a coach, uplifting others, and reminding clients to live their values that sometimes I need someone to reflect my values back to help me see the next right action.

In 2022, I interviewed Amanda Knox, who was released from an Italian prison after four years and exonerated after being falsely accused of murder. She is now a journalist, author, and host of multiple podcasts (check out the *Labyrinths* podcast in particular; it is one of my favorites).

In our conversation, we talked about belonging and advocacy.[15] I asked her how she prioritizes herself, and she said she's a craft geek and likes to make things. Then she asked me what I geek out on. In my podcast I'm usually the interviewer, not the one being interviewed. Her question gave me space to reflect in real time.

My answer was indoor rowing, and I confessed I'd always wanted to row on a real boat but hadn't yet. She asked why I hadn't yet, and I told her that I hadn't tried out of fear of not liking it. What if I had been romanticizing it? That limiting belief was keeping me from trying something new that I had been thinking about for years. Years!

How many times have I avoided trying something because I was afraid I wouldn't like it or wouldn't be great at it? So many times.

Instead of staying course with the status quo, I needed to expand.

I wish I could tell you that I went out and rowed on the water the next day. In reality, it took several months to act—even after I received an email about upcoming rowing sessions. I tried my best to find someone to go with me. I emailed several of my indoor rowing friends, but many had summer plans that would conflict or didn't have the same urge as I did to get out on the water.

So, I did a thing I almost never do. I signed up and went *all by myself.*

That first morning, I arrived at the boathouse when it was still dark outside. Guess what happened? Everyone was nice and very welcoming. And they were all new to rowing on the water. We had that in common.

Even though I had the intention and dream of my plan, I didn't execute it for five years. My advice to you is do the thing you want to do even if it takes more than five years to do it. Have you only been maintaining status quo for one of your values? Where might you need to expand?

In expanding my lens around my value of growth and putting myself into an uncomfortable situation of trying out something new, I found a new team of people that had similar goals to mine. Even though I showed up to the boathouse by myself, I was surrounded by people who shared the same goals and values. We quite literally were in the same boat working in unison on the same goal: to move that boat in synchronization with each other.

To be in sync with a group, you need to find intentional points of connection. In rowing, it is moving on the water. At work, it is through individual conversations, celebrations, and shared experiences with your team. You play an integral part of those intentional moments.

The next section of the Values First Framework is Uplifting Others. Uplifting others is an inherent part of leading a team. In this section, you'll learn the common mistakes leaders make when recognizing team members, how to uplift individuals, and strategies to celebrate and uplift the team.

At an individual level, how do we recognize each other, connect, and celebrate each other's individuality and successes? How can you do that in alignment with the team's values?

COMMON MISTAKES LEADERS MAKE

I once had a leader ask me, "Doesn't everyone think about leadership and their teams this way? With a people-centered approach?"

"No," I said. "Sadly, they don't."

Too often, leaders are driven by results. They have lots of intentions to do right by their team, but at the end of the day, they succumb to the pressures of the business and resort to the actions they are incentivized to do. Most likely, they are incentivized by the results of the work, not by how it gets done.

Here are a few examples of common mistakes. What else would you add to this list from your own experience?

- Not prioritizing care for themselves and in turn setting a bad example for their team
- Incentivizing the wrong behaviors that aren't linked to team values
- Only incentivizing results
- Spending too much time on business, and not enough on people
- Not developing themselves as a manager
- Saying that they are focused on the team's success, but only recognizing an individual's outcome

Before you can uplift individuals on your team or the collective team, you need to set up ways that you are supporting yourself. In the last section of the book, you did this by prioritizing boundaries for yourself. How can you hold yourself accountable to those priorities to care for your values? The good news is that you don't have to do it alone. This chapter is called "Row, Row, Row Your Boat" for a reason. We are starting with you. Your boat.

INDIVIDUAL REFLECTION

You can build a system to include the right people who will help you navigate your values journey. While this is an individual exercise for you to prioritize for yourself as a leader, I want you to invite others to row alongside you. Think of it as rowing solo but having other boats close by, all moving in the same direction. By building and utilizing your Catch Crew, your peer group, you can get the support and accountability you need.

In *Values First*, I describe how to build a Catch Crew with people who can hold you accountable to your values, give you support, and cheer you on. In your accompanying workbook, I want you to revisit your Catch Crew with the Catch Crew Actions Worksheet.

Think of this as a system you are building to support you on your values journey. What topics do you need support on as you continue in this journey? Who else can you include in your Catch Crew to get that support? What boundaries can they help you with most?

By building systems to support yourself, you're setting yourself up for success and modeling that for your team. Without supporting yourself, you will be up the creek without a paddle—in a difficult situation with little chance of positive outcome. You won't be able to help yourself or your team when they need you.

uplifting individuals

When I think about my favorite managers across my career, they had multiple things in common. They valued me. They listened to me. They empowered me. They trusted me. They had tough conversations with me. They challenged me. But most of all, they really knew me.

I get to work with senior leaders who lead teams both big and small. I work with leaders who have been managers for decades, and I get to train leaders who have just become managers for the first time. The best managers I've seen are the ones who are connected to their direct reports.

They meet with them regularly. They build trust with each direct report as individuals. They empower their teams. They build trust in the team by building connection. The good managers listen more than they talk. How do they do this? They prioritize their time with their direct reports.

Let's think about how much time a leader spends with their people versus in the business. The best leaders I know don't default to spending time in the business. They default to spending time with their team. They are spending at least half of their time with their people, sometimes more. You may be thinking, *how can an executive spend more time with their people than on the business?*

Easy: because they trust and empower their teams to get stuff done.

I think leaders always have room to become better managers, whether they've been a manager for decades or have just become one. I have five go-to questions that I think enable more connection between managers and direct reports. If you don't know the answers to these, it is easy to find the answer by spending time with your direct reports and ask them these questions directly.

🚣 TEAM REFLECTION

Go to your Values First Teams Workbook to use the Five Questions Worksheet with your direct report in an upcoming connection.

Here are the top five questions you should ask your direct report to build connection:

1. How do you like to be recognized?
2. How do you like to give and receive feedback?
3. How do you like to learn?
4. What are your values?
5. What's most important for your well-being right now?

Let's go through each of them in further detail.

HOW DO YOU LIKE TO BE RECOGNIZED?

Some people do not care about recognition, but others do! It may be their highest motivator. It is human nature to recognize people how we like to get recognized.[16] But that is a mistake.

If you like recognition, you may recognize people in very open forums. Not all people like that. Some like to be recognized with a personal note, some like to be carbon copied (CCed) on an email. If you don't personally like or need recognition, you may not be recognizing others at all. You may not even realize that you aren't. In fact, it may seem inauthentic to do it. If you need to, schedule it in. It isn't inauthentic; it is being intentional. I don't care if it feels forced for you; the people who like to be recognized won't think that. They will see that you are trying. So schedule in time to recognize others how they like to be recognized.

HOW DO YOU LIKE TO GIVE AND RECEIVE FEEDBACK?

To have trust, you need to build a culture of feedback. Let's start with receiving feedback. How do they want feedback? A quick side conversation after a meeting? A bulleted email list? This isn't just feedback for improvement, but feedback for reinforcement too! How do they like to give feedback? Do they need time to think through it? Do they need to be given a heads-up when feedback is requested?

Giving feedback isn't always easy. Here is a tool that can help you. Whether you are already a pro or you are reluctant, this tool will prepare you to give more positive reinforcement and feedback for improvement.

You already know that I love a good acronym. This is another example of a great one. CARE stands for "Context," "Action," "Result," and "Empower." Here are the steps of the CARE feedback method, a supporting model to the Values First Framework.

Context: What is the context? What happened?

Action: What actions and behaviors have you seen that are or are not in alignment with the team's values?

Result: What is the result of their actions? What was the impact?

Empower: How can you empower them to act in alignment with the team's values?

Use the CARE Feedback Worksheet in your Values First

Teams Workbook to prepare for the next time you'll give feedback for recognition or improvement.

HOW DO YOU LIKE TO LEARN?
Some people love conferences, reading, and podcasts. Some thrive on formal certifications or programs. Some people hate those things. Getting another business book may feel more like a punishment to them than a reward. It feels like more work. Instead, maybe they would love to learn through shadowing someone or diving into a new experience where they can learn on the job. Whatever it is, figure out how each direct report likes to learn and how you can support them in that way.

WHAT ARE YOUR VALUES?
What matters to them? Knowing their values will connect to so many other topics on how to support them. Remember that values can change over time, or one value may be more important than others in certain seasons of life. Knowing which values are most important in this season is vital for you to support them. What value is most important to them right now? Is that being met? How can you help?

WHAT'S MOST IMPORTANT FOR YOUR WELL-BEING RIGHT NOW?
This may mean exercise, nutrition, getting more sleep, more quality time with family, or taking Friday afternoons off. How can you support what they need most? Additionally, what is most important for your well-being right now? Ensure that you model that for them. You and your team should be meeting well-being goals.

AS A BONUS, ANOTHER QUESTION I LOVE TO ASK: HOW CAN I SUPPORT YOU? OR WHAT SUPPORT DO YOU NEED FROM ME TODAY?

This should be a two-way street: have a conversation and share your answers to these questions with your direct report. Listen to their responses. Think of all the things you can learn about each other.

If your manager hasn't asked you these things, don't let that stop you from sharing them with your manager. Tell your manager that you want to start bringing in questions to your one-on-ones or team meetings. Start with one question per team meeting, then open it up with a team connection exercise. Then, over the course of several weeks, you will know so much more about your manager and your team.

In your Values First Teams Workbook, utilize the Five Questions Worksheet for each of your direct reports. How will you put these questions in action? One way is to ask them in your one-on-ones.

Set expectations with your direct reports and let them know that you'd love to incorporate asking more questions in your one-on-ones. Give them the worksheet in advance to fill out and share your answers to the questions with each other. You can do this in one meeting or over several weeks by sharing your answers to the questions one question at a time.

Do this for each of your direct reports to create more connection and trust. Take notes during the meeting. Literally write down what they tell you. You don't want to hear their answers one time; you want to be able to incorporate their answers in how you lead and manage them later. For instance, when you understand how someone likes to be recognized, you can then recognize them in the way that they prefer. This will take you knowing, remembering, and putting their preferences into practice.

It's not enough to just have the information. You need to put the information into practice. Don't just ask the question. Pay attention to the answer and act on it. This will help you stay aligned with team values, keep your team and individual boundaries, and uplift your team members.

Once you've got that alignment between team members, let's learn more about ways your leadership behaviors can uplift your team collectively.

uplifting everyone

So far we've focused on setting up support for yourself and on uplifting individual members of the team. Next, we'll dive deeper into how to maintain your team culture by incentivizing the behaviors you want to see.

The team has already done the work in defining the behaviors that will build and keep the team culture. Now the hard work comes in: living those values consistently. You've already evaluated the strengths and gaps of the team in the Audit Time section of the Values First Framework. There may be some values that the team is already living very consistently. There may be some that need more work.

Remember, the overall culture is built by the behaviors we see and do as a team. Not what we say we will do, but what we actually do. Let's talk about the most powerful ways to reinforce our culture: 1) the behavior of the leader and 2) the behaviors that are rewarded and incentivized.

MODEL TEAM VALUES AND BEHAVIORS

"Do as I say, not as I do" is unfortunately a common philosophy that many leaders live without realizing. Often leaders take on more work to help or protect their team. They shield their teams from seeing things they shouldn't see, like organizational red tape, politics, and poor decision-making.

Often these things take up the leader's time, extend their workday, and lead to working and answering emails at all hours of the night. As leaders, we hope that we do a pretty good job covering up for these things. We hope our teams don't realize that we are checking email on vacation or doing our project work over the weekends when we finally get the thinking time to do it. But guess what? Leaders are not as great at this as we think. Our teams know that we are overworked, overscheduled, and overcommitted. They don't see everything, but they see more than we realize.

What are they seeing? Maybe your lack of boundaries? Your physical presence in the office? You trying to keep up with everything? I was recently talking to a senior leader in a coaching engagement, and she talked about how she fell into the trap of comparing herself to others and wanted to work on it. She mentioned that sometimes she sees that her manager, who is in the C-suite, is still in the office, and she doesn't want to leave before him. So she stays later. She wants to be seen as a strategic, hardworking professional who is loyal and committed to her role. She compared her own hours in the office to her manager's and wanted to show her visible commitment to her role by being there longer than him.

I asked her, "What is that behavior saying to your direct reports?"

She said, "I was so busy thinking about how to manage up that I hadn't even thought about the impact to my direct reports. But they know that they don't have to stay as late as me."

"How do they know that?" I asked.

"I've told them that individually and as a team before," she said.

"But what does your behavior tell them?"

"That I care about staying as late as my manager. So they

probably do the same. I can't believe I've never thought about it like this."

That's the thing. It's usually never intentional. This leader is a high performer, has high potential, and has gotten rave reviews from her direct reports. But guess what else her direct reports know? That she's very busy. That she's potentially overworked. They hope she can sustain herself. How do I know this? Because I interviewed them as her coach. They see more than she realized. Part of her action plan became to intentionally do more for herself and leave earlier because she knows the power of modeling those behaviors for her team.

You don't have to be perfect, but I do want you to be intentional. Are you living the behaviors of your team values? What can you do to model one of those behaviors better and more visibly for yourself and your team?

REWARDING AND INCENTIVIZING BEHAVIORS

I was hired to consult with the senior leaders of a technology company to facilitate a senior leadership team off-site. They had recently acquired a competitor and had rolled out a unified vision and mission. The legacy company had a centralized model with a hybrid work environment. Each employee came to work three days a week with flexibility to work from home the other days. The acquired company had a predominately decentralized workforce that was 80 percent remote. They had one office location, and some of the senior leaders and most of the employees worked from home.

The new senior leadership team was made of leaders from both companies. The CEO was based in the legacy company's headquarters, as were a few of his previous direct reports. We were at the senior leadership off-site—a location with a beautiful view of the water in the distance—when, during a break, I heard the CEO speak to one of his direct reports. "I was in the office on Saturday, and I ran into Thomas. He was the only other person there. I need to get him a gift card."

As I poured my coffee, I couldn't help but notice that a few of the other direct reports made eye contact and rolled their eyes. There was obvious tension as an output of the story the CEO had just told. I had a feeling that this behavior was something that the legacy company valued, but the newly-acquired company didn't. Working over the weekend in the office was something the CEO personally valued, but no one else did.

If a leader's informal or formal recognition is misaligned with the team's values, it is reinforcing and incentivizing a different culture than intended. In this example, the CEO wanted to reward someone coming into the office and working hard on a Saturday. This rewards going above and beyond for the company. By rewarding that behavior, he would be rewarding a culture of working over the weekend and working in person. What about others that may have worked over the weekend but work remotely or in a different office? What if workers got their work done in a different way over different hours?

THE CULTURE IS THE BEHAVIOR THAT YOU ALLOW

What kinds of cultures would be created if these behaviors were allowed or went unchecked? For example:

- An inappropriate joke is shared and everyone remains silent.
- A leader has too many drinks at a company event and shares too much information about a peer.
- A leader has been told they will get a promotion every quarter for the last year, but their efforts continue to go unrecognized.
- A return-to-office policy that some senior leaders

enforce with their teams but most senior leaders ignore because they do not agree with it (and have only voiced this to their teams).
- A leader who blames a peer for missteps and takes sole credit for wins.

If I asked you for more examples, I'm sure it wouldn't take long to come up with many.

The culture is the behavior that is allowed. It is the behavior that you reward and celebrate. The culture is what gets paid and the stories that you tell. The things that get rewarded and retold are things that hold value in the culture.

I want you to reward and recognize behaviors that are aligned with the culture that you want and your team values.

I want you to think about the ways in which you are rewarding your team. Go to your Values First Teams Workbook and review the Team Rewards and Recognition worksheet.

INDIVIDUAL REFLECTION
First, answer the questions on informal rewards and recognition.

- What ways do you reward your team informally? For example, highlighting behaviors in team meetings, celebrating work milestones like work anniversaries, or personal milestones like graduations or birthdays.
- Who do you give most of your time to? Who do you share opportunities with? Who do you go to lunch with most often? Who do you share information with first? Is this equitable across your team? You may not think of this as an informal reward, but it absolutely is. Your direct reports want your time; it is a valuable commodity.
- What actions conflict with the team's values? How can you stop doing them?

Next, think about formal rewards and recognition.

- Do you have a team award? What is the award based on? Who has gotten it the last few awards cycles?
- How can your team award incorporate the team's values and behaviors? What changes do you need to make to reward the behaviors from the team's values?
- What do you need to stop rewarding that is currently in conflict with the team's values?
- Does your department have a departmental award? Have you nominated your direct reports for this award? What is that award based on?

TEAM REFLECTION

Next, bring in the team to make some collective decisions about rewards and recognition. What do they want to see?

Remember, your perspectives aren't the most important here. Building a rewards and recognition program for the team can be very motivating. How can you delegate the rewards and recognition program so that you aren't the only one in charge of it?

Which values are most important to recognize and reward?

What rewards will you prioritize?

How often will you recognize those behaviors?

Your team culture is what you actually reward both informally and formally, not just what you *say* you reward. By reinforcing the behaviors that align with your team values, you are celebrating the team culture that you want: a team culture that will not only uplift your team, but it will also get you the results you want.

strategies to grow

As I learned to row as part of a crew, there were several strategies we used to start our time on the water. One strategy was warming up using pick drills. Pick drills separate or break down the movements of the stroke to warm up.

We would start by rowing with arms only for several strokes. Then we would add in more movement with our torso and finally get to a full stroke by adding our legs. Altogether, this would do the work of moving the boat.

By doing the drills and repetitive movements, we built a strong foundation of our individual strokes. By bringing individual movements of each rower together, we became a unified crew. These intentional strategies made us individually better, but also collectively as a crew.

The next strategies we'll discuss serve the same function as a pick drill. They are strategies that need to be practiced intentionally and are tied back to your foundational job as a leader: to uplift your team. These strategies can be used to increase the collective competencies, skills, and abilities to uplift others:

- Prioritize your team's development
- Have development conversations
- Provide visibility for your team formally and informally
- Model your own professional development for your team

Prioritize your team's development. One way to recognize leaders and uplift them is to prioritize their development. There are leaders that are great at building the capabilities of their teams. There are also leaders that do not prioritize team development. I'm assuming that you are not the latter, as you wouldn't be reading a book on how to build a great team culture.

One way to prioritize your team's development is to budget for it. I'm not talking about giving them time to build a new skill. I'm talking about funding their development opportunities. How much of your budget are you setting aside for team and individual development? How much are you tapping into development opportunities?

INDIVIDUAL REFLECTION

Go to your Values First Teams Workbook for your Team Development Budget Checklist. I want you to plan for the investment of your team within your annual budget. There are some budget lines that you may need to plan for if you don't already have them. They should include the following line items:

- Recognition. How are you going to budget to recognize your team? Informal gift cards? Formal recognition gifts? Experiences together either virtually or in person? Meeting up for the first time for a team off-site and planning something fun for the team to do together?
- Team development. How will your team develop together? What do you need to collectively grow? A skill? A class? A book? Hold a training or workshop for your team or put your team through the Values First Leader Workshop and certification (learn more at TheCatchGroup.com/ValuesFirstWorkshop).
- Individual development. How are you investing in each

person in your team? Some companies have an annual allowance per person, and some have guidelines by level of employees on how much you can spend. Whatever the formula, allocate an amount of money per person. You can also allocate based on their individual development plans. This might look like finding group coaching, leadership coaching, an online course, or conference attendance for each person on the team. I've seen companies that don't offer development for administrative professionals or certain other departments. I think that's a mistake. You should be developing everyone on your team regardless of title. Assign a line item to it. And I get it, your budget may not be that big. But there is something you can do for each team member that is equitable and will help them build their professional skills.

- Your development. One of the best things that you can do for your team is to continue to develop for yourself. How are you budgeting for your own development? Investment in a coach or development program for yourself may be the best gift you ever give your team because you'll show up better for them. Whose budget allocates funds for your development? Your own? Then plan for it. If it is your manager's budget, then ensure they've added a line item.
- Diversity, equity, and inclusion (DEI). You may not own this holistically, as it may be owned by the chief diversity officer or your HR department, but what are you doing to further the diversity, equity, and inclusion for your own team? Is it specific development for underrepresented groups? Is it sponsoring an event for an employee resource group and attending as a team? If it doesn't have a line item, then it isn't getting prioritized. So, make a line item in your budget.

Have development conversations. Have frequent conversations about development with your team. This may be a part of your goal-setting process at the beginning of the year. Don't let that be the only time when their development comes up. Have development conversations quarterly with direct reports in their one-on-ones.

Listen first. When a direct report or team member comes to you for development requests, be curious. Sometimes we have a knee-jerk reaction of answering "no" for budget requests that aren't planned. Listen first. What could be possible? Is the program aligned with their development plan? Is it possible to fund it in the next budget cycle?

More than once I've heard from leaders whose direct reports have asked to go to certification programs for things that didn't really align with their roles. Their managers didn't see the connection. Those employees may have left disappointed and undervalued. I encourage leaders to ask questions like "What do you want to get out of the experience?", "How will that help your current and next role at the company?", and "Is there a mutual benefit for you and the company if you obtain this certification?"

If the person wants to go to an offering but currently isn't performing in their role, you may need to give them that feedback. Use the CARE feedback method to share real-time feedback, set expectations, and empower better performance. They first need to prioritize meeting expectations for their role before adding any other skillsets to their job (unless that is related to the gap in performance).

Provide visibility for your team formally and informally. There are times in succession planning or talent planning meetings when you are talking talent with peers or are in end-of-year conversations where you can advocate for your team to get them merit increases or opportunities for coaching or leadership programs. It is your job to use those opportunities and ensure you are providing visibility for your direct reports and extended team. I've been in these meetings as a leader speaking up for my team and also as a human resource (HR) leader as a facilitator of the conversation. There are some leaders who do this really well. There are some leaders who don't, so get better at providing visibility for your team. This is part of your job as a leader in all spaces you are in.

What spaces am I talking about? Any place that you are that your people are not present, informally or formally. Informally, that may be committee meetings, a conversation with a peer, a skip-level meeting with your manager's manager. How can you highlight the accomplishments of your team in those places? Formally, that may be end-of-year talent discussions with your peers and manager or talent succession meetings. Your role is to talk about the strengths, opportunities, and career aspirations of your team as their representative. Don't be a poor representative in those rooms.

Once, in a talent review meeting I attended, a leader described how he wanted to give top ratings to each of his team members based on their performance. Everyone on his team deserved an above-average rating, he explained. In that moment, he wasn't a very good representative for his team. There was a poor performer on his team, and he wanted to give them the same rating as another, higher-performing team member. By proposing the same ratings, he was doing everyone on his team a disservice. His proposed ratings were challenged, and through discussion and feedback, more accurate ratings were given based on performance. However, he hadn't fully prepared, and instead of using the opportunity to highlight his top performers and give them more visibility, he spent his time defending the poor performer.

Get better at providing visibility for your team in both the informal and formal places.

Model your own professional development for your team. I want you to be transparent about what you are working on for development. If you have a coach or if you are going through a development program, tell your team about it. They won't know what's possible if you don't model it yourself.

Through the Uplifting Others section, you've built in dedicated time for connection for everyone on your team, identified ways to prioritize your team's development, and built some ways to informally and formally reinforce the values-based culture you want to maintain.

I could have stayed in my comfort zone and rowed alone on my rowing machine. But there is a different kind of satisfaction when you and your team are all in sync in the same boat and rowing in the same direction.

As my rowing coach says, "One team, one boat, one goal."

Even if you are rowing in the same direction, sometimes the waters can be rough with strong winds. That's why, in the next chapter, we'll cover how to utilize your team values to navigate conflict.

experiencing conflict

Design how your team will resolve conflict, give feedback, and know how to move forward in alignment with team values.

Values First Teams Workbook tools in this section:
- High/Low Worksheet
- Values Conflict Worksheet

internal conflict

Have you ever been so confident that something will go well and then you are immediately humbled by a different reality? That's how I felt when I started rowing on the water.

I had excelled at indoor rowing for years. It was something I was good at, and proud of being good at. I thought that would translate to the water easily. I had been told by experienced rowers in my indoor rowing classes that I would be great at rowing on the water.

I thought wrong. My simulated rowing was, in fact, not the same as the real thing.

I had been indoor rowing using the same form for ten years. Unknowingly, I'd exaggerated my rowing form by overextending my arms at the catch and leaning back too far after the drive. On a rowing machine, that may be helpful because you have a longer stroke and "travel" more meters. However, it does not translate the same on the water.

I had to unlearn my form, something that I had done over and over for ten years. That's a lot of muscle memory to unlearn.

The thing that I thought would benefit me most on the water—my ten years of indoor rowing experience—put me at a disadvantage.

This was a big point of tension for me. I had to unlearn my indoor rowing form and then relearn the right form. I had to let go of the version of myself that I've had in my head; my idea of the kind of rower I was had to fall away. Reconciling that in my mind was a tension and a conflict that I worked through. I had to remind myself that my core value of achievement wasn't the one to focus on in this moment. Instead, I was living out my core value of growth.

Amy Porterfield, an online entrepreneur, describes how she grew as an entrepreneur on her podcast *Online Marketing Made Easy*. In one episode, she mentions the idea of being uncomfortable in growth.[17] When you are uncomfortable, you are growing and learning. That's what was happening: I was feeling the tension and conflict.

This conflict wasn't an external one. It was an internal one: it was the tension between my core values of achievement and growth. My internal conflict left me frustrated that I wasn't excelling like I thought I would. Externally, it looked like I wasn't synchronized with the other people in the boat. It meant I got more individual coaching while we were rowing.

In this space of discomfort and growth, I wasn't alone. I was being observed by a rowing coach who was watching, guiding, and teaching us from the coaching launch, a motorized boat coaches use to ride alongside rowers. I wasn't the only person who was getting coached either. Everyone received coaching. We also received positive reinforcement. Coaching isn't just about correcting.

I also benefited from the coaching directed at the other members of the crew. I absorbed the feedback and put it into immediate practice. I received encouragement and support from my fellow crew members. I learned the most from them and from their experiences in the boat alongside me.

When you are rowing, you can't see where you are going. You row backwards, only seeing where you've been and not where you are going. You trust each other and your skills to head in the right direction. When one of you faces conflict or tension, you bring it in the boat with you. The tension that I brought with me in the boat could impact the whole crew.

COMMON MISTAKES WHEN EXPERIENCING CONFLICT

Assuming that all conflict is bad. Healthy conflict is necessary in a team environment. Often our first impulse is to avoid conflict, minimize it, or try to resolve it as quickly as possible. I'd like you to think of a conflict as a signal. It could be a signal of values misalignment or an indication of which value is not being met. It could be a signal that you need to pay more attention to a certain value. Processing through conflict can be a way to bring ease and connection, especially within your team.

Wanting results too quickly. I fell headfirst into this mistake when I started rowing. I wanted results too quickly. I was impatient. I see the same thing play out with leaders at work. We have high standards and high expectations. We need patience too.

Minimizing conflict before it is too late. Sometimes you want to give others the benefit of the doubt. You give them multiple chances. You may delay giving them feedback on their performance. By the time you do address the conflict, it may have reached the point of no return. Our fear of conflict is, at times, bigger than the conflict itself. Thinking about possible scenarios, playing out what could happen, ruminating about the situation, and delaying difficult conversations are all normal.

Taking too much responsibility. You may be taking on more than you should as a leader. You may think that it is your job to keep the peace or make everyone comfortable. Unknowingly, you may be creating more conflict by not holding others accountable.

Not owning your part in the conflict. When you are entrenched in conflict with another person, it is very easy to focus on the other person's actions: what part they played and how you are impacted. Often, we overemphasize their role and underestimate the part we play in the situation. We don't take the time to reflect on it, take accountability for it, or act on it.

Sharing too much with your team. Being in conflict is hard and sometimes lonely. I've seen leaders share too much information with their team regarding conflicts with peers or direct reports. It is important to have a peer set or Catch Crew to connect to. **They are not your direct reports.** By disclosing too much information to direct reports you may be acting in misalignment to your team's values or breaching confidentiality. Instead, schedule time with a trusted Catch Crew friend.

In this section of Experiencing Conflict, we discuss three main types of conflicts:

- Internal conflict
- Conflict between you and someone else
- Managing multiple people in conflict with each other

The tools we'll review will help you with all three, but also have special support for you as a leader to manage conflict within your team. Let's start with managing internal conflict.

I know when I'm feeling conflict because I can feel it in my body. I feel nervous or anxious. I may think too much about the situation. That is a sign for me to pay attention. How do you know when you are in conflict or feel tension? What are your signals?

When I have self-awareness of the conflict, I know I need to dig deeper on the situation. The High/Low Exercise can be used to debrief an individual conflict. It is a way to learn from situations. This promotes continual growth because we are never done learning. It is essentially an after-action review, or what a project manager may call a post-mortem. It's the meeting you have after a project ends to see what you learned from it. How often do you have those after-action reviews? Probably not often enough.

🚣 INDIVIDUAL REFLECTION

I want you to do the High/Low Exercise in the Values First Teams Workbook as self-reflection through a conflict or tension you are facing.

The High/Low Exercise has a series of open-ended questions to reflect on. This is an important exercise that can shift your momentum from backward-thinking to forward-minded. Often internal conflict can deplete your energy and take up mind space.

The first thing on the worksheet is to describe the situation:

What were the highs of that experience?

When were you living your values?

What were the lows of the situation?

When did you feel at your worst, and what was happening at that point?

What is your biggest takeaway to live your values more consistently?

After that, you'll have a lens of the highs and lows of your experience. This will give you insight that can be helpful in managing the conflict. You'll come away with multiple learnings and most likely a few themes.

I want you to use this exercise to continue forward momentum through the conflict. Be sure to link back to your core values so that you aren't drawn into the unease and tension of the conflict. Robin used the High/Low Exercise when she was in the messy middle of a career transition.

Robin was a sales executive and one of the only women at her level in the organization. She was often asked to speak on internal career panels to talk about her career journey, sponsor visible change management projects, and speak at events for leadership development within the company. Then one day, Robin was blindsided.

She jumped on a Microsoft Teams meeting with her manager and saw the chief human resources officer on the call. This was an immediate red flag for bad news she wasn't expecting. She was laid off as a part of an organizational restructure where they would be combining regions and thereby reducing the number of senior employees. She hadn't seen this coming.

This wasn't a performance issue. She was delivering results. Her team was too. Who else would be impacted from her team? When would her last day be? How would it be communicated to everyone? Her mind was racing.

Her transition out of the organization would be fast—that week in fact. They said it would be better for the organization. She reluctantly signed her name on the electronic signature page of a generous severance package. And that was it, her time there was over.

I met Robin three months after she left that organization. She reached out because she felt stuck in the tension of how she was let go. Why didn't her manager give her a heads-up? Why her? Why now? She couldn't make sense of it.

In a coaching session, she mentioned that she felt heavy and anchored back into the moment she got laid off. She kept replaying it over in her mind. Was she not good enough? What could she have done differently?

She completed the High/Low Exercise to process that internal tension and conflict. She did it as a reflection exercise on the role, team, and company she left.

What were the highs of her time at the company? She built a great team. She delivered results for the company. She impacted the careers of hundreds of employees through her leadership and by sharing her career experiences.

What were the lows of her time at the company? This one was easy to answer. The way she was let go without warning and without context. She didn't get to make the decision herself; it was made for her.

When was she living her values? She felt that she was living her values of integrity and transparency in the highs and the lows. She was living her value of development when she built her team, gave them feedback, and supported them in their career goals. She delivered results consistently by bringing in revenue for the company, which aligned with her value of growth.

What was her biggest takeaway? She realized that she lived her values throughout her time there and the highs were far greater than the lows. She realized that, by focusing on that one moment in time, she was keeping herself stuck in tension. She was hanging on to this conflict at her own detriment. She knew it was time to let it go and leave it behind. Instead, she would carry herself and her values of integrity, transparency, development, and growth forward to a new experience.

She was able to shift momentum from a conflicted past that she couldn't control to a hopeful future where she would live her values in the next stage in her career. Robin would keep her momentum moving forward by living her values.

Like Robin, we all struggle with conflict, internally and externally. In the next section, we'll talk about how to manage conflict that emerges in relationships with others.

you, me, and conflict makes three

Conflict can be internal, but it often manifests in our relationships with others. Conflict with others sometimes feels loud, defensive, explosive, and overt. It can also feel chronic and needling. Sometimes it is quiet, festering, and drawn out.

In my corporate career, I worked for a global company with regional business units. I led a committee tasked with building the learning strategy for a global function that included senior leader representatives from multiple regions. We met annually in person to discuss the priorities for the year, each representative weighing in on topics that were most important to their respective areas. Many times, there was a high degree of agreement among the members who served on this committee for multiple consecutive years. But there were also some spirited discussions where there were sources of tension.

In one such meeting, I was leading a conversation about a new technology platform that we were deploying at the enterprise level. We had done a successful pilot project in one of the regions, gotten feedback from multiple stakeholders, and were ready to roll it out to all other regions in a cascading plan during the upcoming year. We would be retiring the disparate technology systems that the regions were using now that we had a consistent solution for the company. It would bring efficiencies and save us money, but some regions would lose some existing functionality.

We were reviewing the rollout plan, and the group was in general agreement except for one senior leader. After much discussion, he said, "I'm all in favor of the new system. I get the technology and why it is good for everyone. I'm still not happy that we won't have all the functionality that our people are used to. If we decide to move to the new platform, we'd like to be the last ones to transition to make sure everyone else works through the bugs and hiccups."

"If you decide to move to the new system?" I asked, surprised at the way he had phrased it. I thought he was on board based on some previous discussions and was just getting stuck on the lost functionality.

"I mean, I philosophically agree that we should all be on the same system."

"Okay, so we'll plan for your region in Q4, with regular updates from other regions on our monthly calls. Does that work for you?"

"I'm excited to see how it works for everyone," he said.

As an action item from this discussion, each committee representative would socialize the implementation plans with their respective leadership teams, lead communications to user groups, and prepare to retire their previous systems after the new one was put into place.

This was only one of the action items in our long agenda and we moved on to the next topic.

Fast-forward multiple months and a few regions had implemented the new system and retired their previous systems. We'd met monthly as a committee to keep everyone up to speed on implementation progress, which was going reasonably well with some delays in one region. It was time for the last region to start prepping for their implementation. I asked the senior leader how his region was feeling about their upcoming implementation.

He replied, "Oh, I haven't mentioned it to our leadership team yet. I'm not sure if they are going to be on board at this point in the year."

I was surprised, as we had all agreed to implement the new system in our annual meeting.

I responded with, "I thought you had brought the plan to your stakeholders after our annual off-site. Let's chat after this to come up with a plan."

What had I missed? He had agreed in the annual meeting. Sure, he was hesitant, but he said he philosophically agreed. But he hadn't followed through on our action items.

I caught up with him on the phone later that day. "It was my understanding that we were all on the same page after the annual off-site. We had consensus."

"I do philosophically agree that we should all be on the same system. I just don't think we are ready yet. We had a consensus, but you didn't have my alignment."

I was glad that this was a phone call so he didn't see my eyes roll to the back of my head. I left that phone call more frustrated than when I'd started. "What is the difference between consensus and alignment?" you ask. I had no idea. But what I did know is that this was a conflict. But what was at the root of the conflict?

Sometimes figuring out what is causing the overt or subtle unrest in a team is the hardest thing to do. Often there is a feeling of something being off, something being unsaid, or a feeling of needing to be incredibly careful with words and actions out of fear of another person's response. Other times you know what the conflict is, but the next step of how to resolve the conflict isn't so clear.

To figure out the source of the conflict, we'll utilize a familiar tool—the CARE feedback method—for our values conflict inquiry. The CARE feedback method can be utilized here to ensure we are intentional, thoughtful, and exercising care at points in tension.

Let's dive in more to each part of the CARE feedback method and how we'll use it to get to the root of the conflict:

- Context: What is the context, the situation, and the details around the conflict? What happened, and who was involved?
- Action: Action involves the activities of the individuals in the conflict. What was the individual action that they took? What are the behaviors you saw that were not in alignment with the team's values?
- Result: What was the result of their actions? What was the impact of their behaviors, of not living the values of the team?
- Empower: How can you empower behaviors that act in alignment with the team's values? What behaviors do you need to utilize, and how can you empower others?

I needed to dig into the source of the conflict to understand how to move forward. Otherwise, without all regions onboard, the technology project would fail. Let's break down my conflict using the CARE feedback method.

Context: A standardized technology was needed for a global audience. Each region had different needs and certain regions would lose functionality with the adoption of the new technology.

Action: I moved forward with the project plan assuming consensus. The region representative did not share the rollout plan for the new technology with his leadership team and kept using the existing system.

Result: We both moved forward with our own plans without checking in with each other. Therefore, the project was now off track with no rollout plans for the region prepared. Implications included non-standardized solutions across the company and higher fees for running duplicate technologies.

Empower: To hold everyone accountable to the team decisions, I could have connected more frequently to each region to understand their plans and support them if they got off track.

By carefully thinking through the CARE feedback, the situation becomes about the facts of a situation. When I do this exercise, it helps me depersonalize the outcome. Instead of feeling like I was led astray by my colleague, it becomes apparent that we both proceeded with our own agendas and didn't check in with each other. It also helps me think through how I would empower myself and him in different ways by offering support and finding an outcome that works for all parties.

After multiple conversations, a rework of project deadlines, and some compromise, we were able to bring the leader and his region along in the implementation. However, it didn't happen until the following year.

When you see a behavior in opposition to or deviating from the team values or behaviors, you can recognize it. However, sometimes working teams haven't done this work and have different expectations of what is expected. Thus, unwelcomed behavior goes unchecked. In the previous example, that committee did not have team values to anchor back to.

The good news is that you do have team values to anchor back to, which will help you in conflict resolution. When we have clarity on what the conflict or the root cause is, we can do the next right thing by working through the conflict with the team's values intact.

🚣 INDIVIDUAL REFLECTION

Go to your Values First Teams Workbook and utilize the Values Conflict Worksheet to dive deeper into the conflict. The first part of this exercise enables you to name the conflict. The second part of this exercise helps you dive deeper into the behaviors and outcomes of the situation. The third part empowers you to reflect on the right resolution from the conflict.

1. **Name it**
   a. What values are we not living as a team?
   b. What values are we living as a team?
   c. Where is the tension in the situation?

2. **CARE feedback method**
   a. What is the context?
   b. What actions and behaviors have you seen that are not in alignment with the team's values?
   c. What was the result?
   d. How can you empower behaviors aligned with team values?

3. **Reflection and resolution**
   a. Is the team over-indexing on one team value at the expense of another?
   b. What is the most important team value to prioritize in this situation?
   c. What are the personal accountabilities for each team member involved to live the team values?
   d. What is the next right action for the team and individuals within the team?

After reviewing this exercise as an individual, I want you to use it as a way to create connection with those you are in conflict with.

✐✐✐✐ TEAM REFLECTION

Ensure that all members involved in the conflict or tension do this individual reflection. Then have a conversation with the team members involved to get their understanding of the situation and establish how to utilize the team's values to get back in sync and stay the course.

This exercise can give you the tools you need to name the conflict, depersonalize the outcomes, identify the values and behaviors that are most important to prioritize during conflict resolution, and understand how to empower yourself and others to stay in alignment of team values. From there, you can identify personal accountabilities and how to hold people to their next steps. In that way, you are using the team values and behaviors as a roadmap through conflict.

leader as navigator

As a leader, you'll need to navigate all kinds of conflicts: internal conflict, conflict between you and someone else, conflict with your team, and interpersonal conflict between others. Sometimes the source of conflict isn't you or the team. Even still, you can use the team values to help address conflict and issues that arise.

One of the biggest sources of conflict I've consistently seen over my twenty-year corporate career as a human resource executive and executive coach is the reluctance for leaders to have difficult discussions. Just like there is a meeting culture in a team or company, there is a culture of feedback (or lack thereof).

What is the culture of feedback in your team? Giving or receiving feedback may be an identified behavior in the team values that you've created, but there are a lot of reasons that people don't like to have difficult conversations or discussions. Here are a few:

- They don't want to create more conflict
- They don't want to put someone on the spot
- They don't want to be the bearer of bad news
- They don't want to disrupt the relationship they have with someone
- They don't feel confident in the message
- They don't feel prepared
- They want to give a person the benefit of the doubt

- They don't want to make another person feel bad
- They don't want to receive feedback themselves
- They don't want to give negative feedback to someone who has power or seniority over them
- They don't think the other person is receptive to feedback
- They don't want to be the first one to bring up something negative in front of a group

Whew! That's a lot of reasons to not have a difficult conversation. No wonder we aren't having the kind of discussions that often result in conflict.

When partnering with one senior leadership team, I was debriefing a conversation about priorities and decision rights when the CEO had to leave the room to take a quick call. He had been the CEO for two years, coming in externally after the founder of the company had transitioned. In their senior leadership team, there were some longtime employees and some that were newer. As the CEO left the room, the conversation quickly shifted. The leaders started talking about different things with more candor, more examples, and more agreement.

I asked, "How did we get to this conversation so quickly? What has changed?" Everyone looked at the empty chair the CEO had vacated, with his computer and the remnants of his breakfast still at his place at the table. What went unsaid in that moment: they felt able to talk more freely because the CEO was absent.

"I'm going to bring up the elephant in the room. Why aren't we talking about this with the CEO? What's standing in your way?" I asked.

The new communications director spoke up. "We've tried to communicate the issues with decision rights with him. It feels like a broken record sometimes. We come to an agreement, but then he makes a different decision. What's the point in talking about decision rights when he's going to make all the decisions and be a bottleneck?"

The team felt defeated and disengaged from meaningful conversation with him in the room. They were more open and honest when he wasn't there. The CEO didn't have the self-awareness to understand the situation. He was part of the problem, and the team had some ownership in it too, as they didn't want to give him that feedback in the moment.

We utilized the time in the team meeting to name sources of conflict and isolate the things the team wasn't talking about. Not only did the team have a candid dialogue with the CEO about decision rights—they also named multiple other sources of conflict that they wanted to work through in the future.

I was meeting with a different CEO, preparing for a retreat for her senior leadership team. She mentioned that one struggle that she was having with her team is that she consistently received feedback from one direct report. This direct report was seen as the "spokesperson" for giving feedback to her, as she brought messages from other people on the team. It was a triangulation of feedback. Someone would tell the direct report, she would tell the CEO, and the CEO would address it in the team meeting. It had happened a few times, so she wanted to change the dynamic and really get to the root of the issue.

We decided to tackle it by naming the elephants in the room (i.e., the sources of conflict for the team), knowing that this one would be one of multiple issues that would bubble up. As a part of the introduction to the exercise with the team, I told the same story of the CEO who left the room. The plan was for them to imagine that their CEO wasn't in the room and explore what topics came up for them.

Things didn't go according to plan, but I couldn't have planned it better if I had tried. Not more than twenty minutes later, the CEO had to excuse herself from the room to take a call about an emergency that had surfaced unexpectedly. After generating a few sources of conflict from the team, we started to discuss them. Then one leader said, "Are we going to be really honest here? Can I do that?"

"That is exactly what I'm asking for in this discussion," I replied.

She went on to give an honest opinion of a few issues that impacted multiple members of the team. We went on to have a very robust conversation. And when the CEO came back into the room, we were able to bring her back into the conversation. The issues raised were not about the CEO, but they might not have been addressed at that level of depth if she hadn't left the room. In that team session, we grounded the team back into the behaviors of their values of collaboration and transparent communication.

In that example, the team was performing well, had a few issues with communication, then utilized their team values and behaviors to improve the culture of feedback on their team. The CEO prioritized her team's development by prioritizing this team session. She took intentional steps to prioritize her team's culture. She even took it a step further and used a facilitator so that she could participate in the day and not run the session herself.

Partnering with a facilitator to navigate team dynamics creates a safe space and gives permission to the team to name things that they may not otherwise. This team utilized the Values First Framework to prioritize a culture of feedback. You can too. Go to TheCatchGroup.com/AboutUs to get further information on using a certified Values First facilitator for your next team off-site or retreat.

How can you make progress on your culture of feedback and resolve conflict in the team? I'm not suggesting that you ask the question "When I'm not in the room, what do you talk about?" to your team—you most likely will not get a direct answer. If they aren't talking to you about it with you there, then they probably won't talk about it if you ask either.

Here are a few ideas on how to build a culture of feedback with your team:

- Have confidential processes for individuals to submit ideas (sticky notes, surveys)
- Ensure that everyone has equal time to offer their point of view (give thinking time for those that need it in advance)
- Model giving feedback using the CARE feedback method
- Ask for feedback
- Ask individuals how they like to receive feedback
- Give informal feedback in one-on-ones
- Prioritize positive feedback using the CARE feedback method
- Hold skip-level meetings with people on your team (meeting with your direct report's direct report)
- Ask questions
- Be open to others' opinions and ideas
- Be curious
- Prioritize a team off-site facilitated by a Values First Framework–certified facilitator

Using the team values and behaviors, you can set expectations on how feedback is used to build the team culture and results you want.

WHEN TEAM VALUES COME IN CONFLICT

Often internal conflict arises for me when two of my core values come in conflict with each other. This usually shows up when my value of achievement takes priority, and I find myself working too much. This has come up multiple times in my career. The conflict then arises when I burn out, neglecting my core value of balance.

It isn't an external conflict; it is a tension within two values that are important to me. In some seasons, it may make more sense to over-index on my value of achievement. But usually, even though my habit is to lean into that value, I'm trying to unlearn some of those behaviors and instead lean more into my value of balance.

Unironically, when my value of balance is met, I'm more focused and achieve more because I'm clear, not as stressed, and have met my needs. Through balance, I can be a better leader.

The same internal tension can happen in teams. The conflict comes when a team over-indexes on one core value and ignores another. In one team values workshop, a senior leadership team came together for their annual off-site. They were a decentralized team: some were based regionally and some were based at the company headquarters.

During the Audit Time phase of the Values First Framework, they noted that one of the team's strengths was their core value of compassion. They were thoughtful, kind, and positive leaders. The gap that they identified was within their core value of transparent communication. They wanted to get better and practice this core value more. The behaviors that they defined for transparent communication were engaging in productive conflict, being loyal to decisions, holding each other and the extended teams accountable, and speaking their perspectives with honesty.

They knew that this would be a source of conflict for the team, as their compassion meant that they weren't always transparent with each other. The team brainstormed actions to mitigate this potential conflict including:

- Holding each other accountable to bring up tough conversations
- Inviting each other to share opinions and insights
- When in conversation with a peer and hearing about a new issue that wasn't shared, ask, "Why didn't you feel comfortable bringing it up to the group?"
- Assume positive intent, but share information with peers honestly
- Checking in when their values might conflict with each other

This is a great example of a team being proactive and mitigating potential conflict with actions and behaviors in line with their team values. They know that it's impossible for everyone to perfectly live the team's values all the time, so they have built in support for each other that steers back to the desired team values and behaviors.

During a team values workshop with another client, one participant within a sales department asked an important question. "What happens when it feels like you have to sacrifice your values to meet your goals?"

I asked, "Where is the tension in that situation?"

He replied, "The tension is in our team value of team health. We are working so much, with longer hours, to meet our goal. It feels like there's a trade-off between our health and well-being and meeting our goal."

"How can you live your team value of team health while also being in pursuit of your sales goals?" I asked.

Are these things mutually exclusive? Or is there another way? The team decided to deprioritize nonessential work and bring in a temporary contractor to cover one project so they could focus on the priority project. That provided some temporary relief so that they could focus on their goal while keeping their team values intact.

One team member noted, "There's a bigger risk to not living our value of team health. We could burn out while trying to get this goal. Then that will become the culture: work over our well-being. That's not the culture we want."

Build the culture you want.

To get the results I wanted in rowing and in business, I had to slow down and process the internal and external conflicts before I could do my part in getting the boat to move smoothly.

In this section of the Values First Framework, you tackled how to find the source of conflict in a team, utilized the CARE feedback method to fully understand a team conflict, built a culture of feedback, and use your values to make hard decisions through conflict both as a team and as an individual. In the next section, you are going to build out the plan for sustaining the team's values with intention.

sustaining values

Build an action plan to intentionally sustain your team culture for the long term.

Values First Teams Workbook tools in this section:

- Team Values Sustainability Plan
- Individual Commitment Worksheet

moving forward

I sometimes joke that rowing is the perfect team sport for introverts. When you are in the boat, you are sitting behind someone with your back to someone else. You only see the back of your crewmate's body and head.

You have the benefit of your crew to keep you stable in the boat, but still have your own space to learn, grow, and contribute to the team's success. When I'm in the boat, I feel connected to the crew—but it is also an individual experience because there is no one to make direct eye contact with.

You can't go it alone. It doesn't work in rowing on the water with a crew, and it doesn't work in a values-based team.

How do you stay connected while still moving forward together as a team?

You build a plan: a Team Values Sustainability Plan.

You are on your way to becoming a Values First Team. You've built the foundation with team values and behaviors, set up accountabilities and ways to care for the team's values through team boundaries, and planned for working through conflict with your team values intact. The last section of the Values First Framework is setting up the team for success with Sustaining Values.

Often in business, success is defined as financial growth, increased sales, or an increased customer base. We want to see hard numbers on effectiveness and return on investment. But success doesn't always need to equate to *more* of something. Success in living my values sometimes means working less to ensure that I'm meeting my core value of balance. We need to shift the meaning of success from "more, more, more" to "measuring what matters."

When a team becomes a Values First Team, they benefit from a holistic sustainability plan for their team culture.

Next, we'll set up a Team Values Sustainability Plan, which outlines how we will intentionally spend time devoted to achieving our desired results. By being intentional about our team culture, we'll be building the muscle we need for members of the team to be in alignment with the team's values.

Remember that Venn diagram and the importance of the overlap between individual values and organizational values for values alignment? By spending time on your team culture, you will impact the values alignment and engagement of the individual team members within the team.

TEAM REFLECTION

Let's set up some milestones for the sustainability of the team's values and behaviors. Go to your Values First Teams Workbook to fill out your Team Values Sustainability Plan, which will help you set a plan for what matters most for the team. I recommend doing this exercise as a team to ensure the group builds a plan together and everyone can share thoughts.

You can build this plan together in a team off-site at the beginning of the year or as a finalization of your team values in a separate team meeting. Start with annual activities you will do as a team to sustain your team values and behaviors.

Annual Team Values Sustainability Plan activities

- Start with important check-ins, including the Values Check-In Worksheet to check in on your individual

values, and the Team Values Check-In Worksheet to check in on your team values. How are individuals feeling about how their personal core values are being met? What do they need to celebrate or recalibrate? How do you feel about your team values? What is the group consensus on what you should celebrate or recalibrate? Do you need to tweak any behaviors that align with your team values?
- Audit Time and see where your team values, meeting culture, technology, and processes are aligned. What is working? What needs to be changed?
- Check in on how you are caring for the team's values through your team's boundaries. Are you celebrating your team boundaries consistently? Do you need to shift focus to a new boundary?
- As a leader, ensure consistency in Uplifting Others in your team. Are you conducting one-on-ones regularly? Are you recognizing the accomplishments of team members? Have you formally recognized team members for their contributions aligned with the team's values? How has that been received by the team?
- Allocate next steps to team members for any changes in your meetings, technology, or processes.
- Partner with a certified Values First facilitator for a team culture-building session.

Next, identify the actions that you will take as a team that are quarterly that will build and keep your team culture focused on the team values and behaviors.

Quarterly Team Values Sustainability Plan activities
- Complete and review the Team Values Check-In Worksheet as a team in a team meeting. Rotate the team

member who facilitates this discussion every time you meet.
- As a team, make a list of how you are caring for the team values by sharing examples of recent boundaries you've seen from team members.
- Share examples of how people have celebrated living the team's values as a group.
- Identify how you as a leader have been modeling behaviors for the team. Has it been consistent? Do you need to collect feedback from your direct reports?
- Ensure the team's values is a recurring agenda item on your team meetings.

At the end of a Values First Team off-site, one team was prioritizing their next steps and actions. The leader mentioned, "I don't want this workshop to be something that we did one time and never do anything with. Let's make our plan doable but not too complex."

The team had built the foundation of their team values at the off-site. Next, they established how they would integrate that foundation into their daily work as a team. Here's what they committed to as a team and as individuals for their Team Values Sustainability Plan:

- Attend an annual retreat led by a Values First facilitator to check in on team values and team goals
- Build a meeting culture for bi-weekly team meetings that is aligned with their team values
- In meetings with their direct reports, check in on individual values and values alignment with career conversations
- In quarterly team meetings, add a Team Values Check-In to celebrate and recalibrate

Don't let this work be a one-and-done activity. The only wrong ways to sustain values are not building the sustainability plan at all or not implementing the plan you've built. Here are a few more ideas from Values First Teams:

- All team members to attend the Values First Leader Workshop and receive their certification
- Ensure each team member has a copy of Values First and the Values First Workbook
- Partner with The Catch Group to build and administer a customized Values First Team Pulse Check that will use team members' confidential feedback to measure satisfaction with the team culture, values, and behaviors
- Create visual reminders of team values by having physical printouts, screen savers, or other swag (so long as it doesn't just become words on walls)
- Create a custom award linked to a team value to be awarded quarterly
- Train new team members on the team's values and behaviors
- Share team values with peers and managers to highlight positive culture outcomes

Now you've built a Team Values Sustainability Plan. By building it together, it has increased the likelihood that you'll implement it. But even the best-laid plans sometimes don't get implemented—in the next section, we'll talk about how to create systems that set you and your whole team up for success.

better together

My core value of achievement sometimes gets me in trouble as a recovering perfectionist. I create big plans, and when I don't tick off every box, I'm sometimes inclined to abandon the plan. Don't let that happen to you or your team.

This happened as I learned how to row on the water. I was impatient with my progress. In one lesson my coach said, "Laura, you are trying to correct yourself in the moment, and it is messing up your stroke. Instead, you need to commit to the stroke. You get another chance with every stroke."

I was always trying to do it perfectly, even while I was moving. Instead of trying to be perfect and correcting in the moment, I needed to commit to the stroke and ask myself what would happen if I committed to it, good or bad.

What would happen if you tried something all the way without correcting yourself? There's a freedom in doing something imperfectly.

I want you to move forward in your values journey, as a leader and as a team, imperfectly. Your plan doesn't need to be complex, but you do need to start. And you need to start together.

How are you supporting your team as they start their values journey? Modeling your commitment to the team's values journey is a great way to start.

To be a better crew member in rowing, I took some solo

lessons. Getting better as an individual made me a stronger rower, which made the crew stronger. I learned to row on the water as part of a crew in different-sized boats. The number of crew members in a boat varied depending on the boat size (sometimes there were eight crew members, sometimes four, and sometimes two). In solo lessons, it is just you, two oars, your skiff, and a coach in a boat alongside you supporting you along the way.

Within the first five minutes of my first solo lesson, I almost ran into a dock. Alone, I didn't have the benefit of others to help with stability and navigation. It was all up to me. In that solo lesson, I got so much better as a rower and more skilled as a navigator. I learned different techniques to maneuver the boat. I felt exponentially more confident.

Doing that solo work made me a better crew member when I got into another boat with a crew later that week. My solo work and increased confidence that I brought into the boat made the entire crew better.

Sometimes even the best-laid plans aren't executed because you don't want to mess up or a certain component is too complex. Sometimes it is because of workload or competing priorities. Team members may move on to new teams, or new priorities may emerge.

How do you ensure that you have commitment within your team as you implement your Team Values Sustainability Plan?

⚑⚑⚑⚑ TEAM REFLECTION

Go to your Values First Teams Workbook and review the Individual Commitment Worksheet. This worksheet ensures that the team is growing together and as individuals with accountability in place.

Answer the following questions individually:

- What action item resonates with you from the Team Values Sustainability Plan? Why do you think it is beneficial for the team?
- What action do you not resonate with? What concerns do you have?
- What are you most excited about?
- What will you struggle most with?
- How will the Team Values Sustainability Plan help us reach our team goals?
- What is your individual commitment to the Team Values Sustainability Plan? Will you lead a specific action item? Will you support your team members? Will you give feedback? Be specific.

After completing your Individual Commitment Worksheet, invite everyone from the team to share out their individual commitments with the group. Hearing about individual commitments may inspire team members, motivate through shared goals, and hold the team accountable to building the team culture to get the results everyone wants.

Remember all the tools you have available for you and your team. We've put a list of them at the back of this book for your easy reference. By building an intentional team culture, your team will find greater values alignment in their work. They'll most likely find greater values alignment with their core values as well.

getting results you want

"The regatta is coming up—who's in?"

When I saw the message come through our group chat, my stomach did a little flip. Was it excitement? Anxiety? Both? I purposefully ignored that feeling as I raced to check my calendar to see if it was possible. I wanted the answer to be yes.

The message from my rowing coach was to our rowing crew. She was planning for us to compete in the next regatta—a rowing race—against other crews. Based on who could attend and the events schedule, she would put together boat lineups.

Even though the regatta was just a few weeks away, somehow my calendar was clear. I committed to it. I would be racing for the first time. My stomach tied itself in a knot as soon I committed. That anxiety continued off and on for the next few weeks, increasingly "on" as the day got closer.

The night before, I didn't sleep well. I'd never been so nervous for anything—even high-level presentations and tests hadn't affected me so much.

Will I flip the boat?
Will we finish the race?
Should I even race?
Would they do better without me?

Should I quit and just go back to sleep?

I did not go back to sleep. I grounded myself in my value of growth. When I'm learning, I'm uncomfortable. And I was very uncomfortable. I was exactly where I should be when living my value of growth.

We have people of various levels of experience in our rowing crew. Many of us learned to row on the water within the last few years. We get out on the water or on rowing machines a few times a week, but schedules and injuries dictate who is available to row on which days. This means that, in practice, you are most likely rowing with different people in different boats each time. Rarely do you have a consistent crew and boat for practicing weekly.

That meant that for this first race, although I'd been in a boat with some of the crew, the four of us had never all rowed together. We'd also never rowed in the boat we'd be racing in. Lots of unknown variables were at play, but we were up for the challenge and experience.

How can I describe how my body felt before racing? In one word, *chaos*.

A quad is where four rowers work together to propel a boat. In this event, each of us had a pair of oars, and the boats didn't have coxswains. Quads race against other crews in the same boat type. A race begins with the boats in a stationary position, lined up in lanes across a river with one boat in each lane. From an aerial view, it looks similar to how swimmers line up. At the start, our boat moved quickly with powerful strokes to get the boat moving. About midway through the course, our boat started veering toward the edge of our lane. If you cross the lane, you are disqualified. We took direction from the bow (the rower that steers the quad) to quickly course-correct. Unfortunately, that led to an overcorrection toward the other side of the lane. At that moment, I caught a crab.

In rowing, catching a crab refers to a situation where a rower's oar blade gets stuck in the water, disrupting the stroke and the boat's movement. It's called "catching a crab" because of how the oar behaves—like a crab grabbing hold and not letting go. Catching a crab is often a rower's worst nightmare during a race because it can single-handedly ruin an otherwise well-executed race.

If it is a minor crab and the rower can recover, it will cause a small disruption. If it is a major crab, the oar will get submerged in the water, causing the handle to knock into the rower's body and potentially knock them off the boat. My crab was the latter.

While I successfully remained in the boat, I had gotten knocked pretty badly by my starboard oar. We had to slow down for me to recalibrate. I was able to get back into the stroke, then it happened again—another crab. And then another. It felt impossible to recover.

We finally made it to the finish line within our lane boundaries, but in last place. The crew was mostly silent rowing back to the dock.

I felt horrible. I had let the team down.

I was wet and bruised, but I did not flip the boat.

We'd finished the race, although not the way that we'd wanted to.

I apologized to the team, and they gave me words of encouragement. As we placed the boat back on the rack, the crew noticed that the skeg was slightly tilted. A skeg is a small, fin-like structure located on the bottom of the boat. It plays a critical role in helping the boat move through the water. If it's crooked, the boat won't row in a straight line in the water. That small variation in position most likely contributed to our boat veering off course, which in turn caused my crab and not-so-great recovery from it. That, in addition to my inexperience.

A teammate asked, "Well, how's that for your first race?"

"It sure was an experience," I said.

"At least it is out of the way now. Now your next race will be even better," she said encouragingly. I really hoped that was the case.

My next race was scheduled for the next morning. It would be another quad, but this time with a coxswain on the boat. A coxed four event is where the boat is crewed by four rowers, each with a single oar, and a coxswain who steers the boat and coordinates the crew but doesn't row. Having a coxswain is a benefit for the crew, as they don't have to worry about navigation. The coxswain's job is solely to navigate. While they are an additional person in the boat, they are typically slender in stature and lightweight—therefore adding minimal load to the boat. I'd never been in this formation before, let alone raced using it.

Our crew had some of the same rowers as the day before, but we started out differently the second day. One crew member encouraged us before leaving for the dock. "Let's run our race, not anyone else's. We aren't in competition with anyone. Let's stay connected and be in sync."

The race would be on the same course as the day before, but our crew had more experience and a common goal for the race. We started off quickly, keeping up with another boat. Our boat felt steady, strong, and connected.

About three quarters through the course, I caught a minor crab but was able to recover quickly enough that we didn't lose too much momentum. Eventually the other boat did get to the finish line before us, but we did finish.

"How did that race feel?" asked a crew member.

"It was so great, it felt so much better than yesterday!" I said.

"We raced our race, not anyone else's," said another team member.

Like many races, the outcome of a regatta is measured. It is an outcome that can be tracked. First place, second place, third place, and so on all the way until last place. It also tracked the amount of time it takes a boat to get from the starting line to the finish line.

By objective measures, in both races, we received last place.

Why did the second race feel like a better race? Because we were steady together. Because we were in sync together. Because we got the boat to the finish line without a major or minor disaster. Because it felt good. We were dry. We progressed. We accomplished what we wanted to, but more importantly, we were happy with *how* we did it.

It wasn't even a comparison; the second race was far better than the first race.

Personally, I felt more confident after the second race. I felt accomplished. I felt like I was part of a team. I felt like we did the thing we set out to do.

After getting back home from the regatta, I decided to look up our race times. I wanted to see the official recorded times and figure out how much faster our second race was as compared to our first (even though we were in two different boat types). I was anticipating a big difference in time—the faster time for the smoother second race.

I looked up the time for our chaotic first day and was shocked to see that we'd gotten through the course four seconds faster than we did on the second day. By the usual measure of success—time—we'd done better on the chaotic row.

By every other measure, we had a better row on the second day.

The outcomes we usually measure for success may not be as telling as the real story.

Time didn't tell this story well.

Instead, the real story was in the steadiness of the boat, the feeling of comradery after the race, the comparison to the day before, the growth in confidence that I had, and the sense of owning the experience of rowing our race. All of those things were really the signs of success and growth.

When you measure success, it needs to be based on more than one metric. Especially when you are measuring team success. My individual journey was absolutely part of the team's success and contributed to us having a better second race. My experience with the first race made me better for the second race.

I'd rather be slower with the team and feel amazing about our journey, instead of being faster and in chaos any day.

How are you measuring success for yourself? For your team?

Highly engaged teams with winning cultures lead to winning results. The team needs to row together in the same direction, or else they won't go anywhere. Over time, a team that is in sync can develop into a high-performing team.

In rowing, when a crew finds that moment of high performance in sync, that's called swing. In his book *Swing*, Sigval M. Berg describes swing as "the moment when divergent strength achieves the synchronized harmony of high performance."[18] It is the feeling of being in complete flow, with all of the crew in one mind. All of us together are greater than the inviduals added up and exponentially greater together than an individual standing alone. Everyone finds their rhythm together and moves in the same direction to reach unparalleled success.

How do you define unparalleled success?

- Exceeding annual goals
- Making a large-scale impact
- Getting your dream job

These ideas are big and exciting. These examples are all outcome based. You can measure all these examples. Objectively, once reached, they can't be refuted.

Your team values journey isn't only about the outcome. It is about *how* you got there. Objective measures of revenue growth, increased profit margin, greater efficiencies, or meeting deadlines may not be the best indicators of success.

You've redefined success because you've set the expectations as a team together through your values work. When the team is living the team's values, they will experience swing. For us, swing is the values alignment that each individual feels when there is connection to their individual values, to the team's values, and to the organization's values. Swing is the increased employee engagement, discretionary effort, and sense of belonging that each individual feels by being part of the team.

When someone inevitably catches a crab at an important time, you'll lead with your own values to help them navigate through it, getting them and the team back on course. You'll finish the race, and you will all have grown in the process.

You can use your values to get the life and career you want for yourself and model that for your team members as well. You can build the values-based culture you want without sacrificing results. You now have a Team Values Sustainability Plan that includes annual and quarterly action items along with individual commitments from each team member.

To be in sync on the water, you must be connected to the crew and adjust together. And you must work on yourself. You must be committed to doing both. The same goes for business.

This is the last section of the Values First Framework. Congrats! Now let's talk about where you go from here.

conclusion

keep rowing and growing

Let's celebrate how far you've come in your Values First leadership and team journey!

The Values First Framework gives you a set of tools that you can use for yourself and for your team. It is a journey of growth and development. I want you to revisit your core values and team values often. By leading with your core values, you can show up authentically for your team and empower them to do the same.

Let's summarize your Values First Teams learning journey:

Values First. You identified what matters most to you and built your Values Statement to communicate your authentic leadership to your team. You grew your understanding of what values alignment means for you and for each team member. You prioritized time with your team to build your team values. You got specific with behaviors linked to team values and with what living those values looks like for the team.

Audit Time. You audited how you and your team are currently living up to the team values and behaviors. You further defined the team's meeting culture and prioritized how to align systems, processes, and communications to the team's values.

Life Boundaries: You started by modeling your own boundaries with your team to give them permission to do the same. You established boundaries to show care for your team values and team members and hold each other accountable for the team culture you want.

Uplifting Others: You learned how to support yourself and the individuals on your team through intentional connection. You utilized rewards and recognition systems tied to team values to incentivize the behaviors that will sustain your team culture. You learned strategies to prioritize your team's development.

Experiencing Conflict: You learned how to navigate through internal conflict. You know how to find the source of conflict between you and others. You know how to utilize the team's values to mediate team conflict.

Sustaining Values: You built a customized action plan to intentionally sustain your team culture for the long term and ensure accountability from all team members.

The questions and exercises in this book are designed as tools for you to utilize with your team. You don't have to utilize all of them. You can prioritize the tools that are most important to you in real time and provide your team the tools from this book. You can use this book as a reference guide and share your personal learning with your team and peers. You can also be intentional and use these tools over the course of time.

The best advice I can give you is to actually use the tools in this book. If you've made it this far, I know you've liked the content. But have you done the exercises yet? No judgment if the answer is no! Grab the workbook at TheCatchGroup.com/ValuesFirstTeams.

Your team's culture will be shaped over time. It is up to you to build the team culture that you want—it is entirely within your control. You can intentionally do this work if you prioritize it.

Through this book and workbook, I've laid out a path for you to build a healthy team culture. I'm personally here for you if you need coaching or facilitation support. I'm also here to help you celebrate your progress.

To keep learning from me on a more frequent basis, be sure to follow and share episodes of my podcast, *You Belong in the C-Suite*. Who knows, maybe you'll even be a guest on the podcast in a future episode to talk to me about your experience with these tools. I'd love to share your progress and successes.

The team's values are the foundation of the culture. They aren't written in stone. The team's values can and should evolve over time, just like the team. Your team will not be the exact same people in the exact same positions forever.

The first time I went out on the water with a crew, we didn't move very fast. We were moving so slowly that the coach said he saw a dead fish float by us. After several weeks of working together, we progressed—finally in sync.

Your team values journey will be the same. At first, you may not move very fast. You may even see tensions rise as you work toward new behaviors as a team. But over time and with intentional work, you'll start to see progress.

One morning, the crew was getting ready to take an eight-person boat out. There was one problem: we only had seven rowers. Can you still row with a rower missing? I found out that yes, in fact, you can. But it is harder.

We had to shift our strategy. We moved people around to ensure we had stability. I had to change seats and row in a new position. One of the seats sat empty, but the boat was stable.

As a leader of a team, sometimes you must shift your strategy too. You can use your team values to stabilize your boat.

When someone is missing in a team at work, some of the same behaviors emerge:

- You need to reassign work
- You will have new expectations
- You will most definitely still feel the "empty seat"
- The team has to work together differently, and the result most likely won't be the same

The biggest lesson I learned when rowing with one person missing was that you can still get the boat out on the water. However, the boat weighs more with one less person carrying and supporting it out of the water and back to the boathouse.

As you build your Values First Team, inevitably, you'll have an "empty seat" on the team. That should be a goal of yours as a leader: to support your team so well that they move on in their careers to new opportunities, new roles, and new experiences for growth. Part of leading a team is leading through these transitions. You can do that with your team values intact.

In all transitions, remember to ground yourself in your own core values. As you and your team grow and evolve over time, ground your team in the team's values. You'll inevitably bring in new team members to the existing team culture. Include new members in the development and evolution of your team culture—by inviting them to participate, new members will feel included and involved. Welcome them into that team culture and evolve together.

By building a Values First Team, you are building the culture you want without sacrificing results. Your Values First Team culture will impact not only the lives and careers of your team but will leave ripples within your organization.

I cannot wait to hear about the impact of the team cultures you'll create and the leaders that you'll inspire. The growth that will happen won't just be yours or your team's. Growth will spread more broadly because of how you've modeled your values consistently in times of high performance and in high conflict.

And who knows, maybe you've been inspired to get into a boat and get out on the water. There's nothing like it. No rests, no pauses, only a small recovery before the moment of connection at the catch. The catch is just before the change of direction. It is the moment before you drive back with the power of your legs, lats, and torso: a moment of connection, then a chance to start again with each stroke.

In rowing and in leadership, you always get another chance to start again. Start with your values first.

values first teams workbook tools

Values Worksheet—to gain clarity on what matters most. Use this annually to gain clarity and ground yourself in your values.

Values Check-In—to revisit your values and check in on how you are feeling about them showing up in your life. Use this quarterly and share with your manager or team.

Values Alignment Worksheet—to evaluate how your core values align with the organization's values. Understand your personal values alignment and how your team is aligned with the organization's values.

Values Statement Worksheet—to share your values and how you lead with your values. Share this with your team in one-on-ones and weave in stories about your values to consistently talk about them.

Building Connections Tool Kit—to learn about each team member's core values in a team connection exercise.

Team Values Worksheet—to identify what matters most to the team and how to live the values with specific behaviors.

Team Values Check-In—to check in on how you are individually living the team's values and on how the team is living values collectively. Identify strengths and gaps.

Values First Meetings Worksheet—to ensure the team is intentionally aligned on team values and behaviors as you meet and work toward your goals.

Team Systems and Processes Audit—to identify which systems and processes are aligned or misaligned with your team values.

Build a Boundary Worksheet—to prioritize boundaries aligned with your core values and model that behavior for your team to give them permission to do the same.

Team Boundary Worksheet—to build collective boundaries and accountabilities to show care for your team values and each other.

Catch Crew Action Worksheet—to create the support system that you need to uplift yourself and your peers.

CARE Feedback Worksheet—to give feedback for reinforcement or improvement to empower your team's growth.

Five Questions Worksheet—to build connection with individuals on your team to ensure you understand their needs and what support they need.

Team Rewards and Recognition Worksheet—to incentivize the behaviors you want to build and keep in the team culture, both formally and informally.

Team Development Budget Checklist—to prioritize your team's development and growth year after year.

High/Low Worksheet—to debrief a tough situation individually or with a team. Use this often to resolve internal or external conflicts.

Values Conflict Worksheet—to find the source of conflict, tie it to a team value or behavior, and manage it through conflict resolution.

Team Values Sustainability Plan—to take intentional action to build a Values First Team culture with individual commitment to next steps.

Individual Commitment Worksheet—to state your personal commitment to living the team values and behaviors.

Values First Framework from *The Catch Group*

LEADER

TEAM

ORGANIZATION

To get the free Values First Teams Workbook, go to TheCatch-Group.com/ValuesFirstTeams. Take action to build the team culture and results you want.

frequently asked questions

Through my Values First Framework over the past few years—coaching clients, collaborating with organizations, and speaking to in-person and virtual audiences—I've talked to countless leaders about values. There are similar themes that have bubbled up. In this section, we'll cover some of those themes.

DO VALUES CHANGE OVER TIME?

What is a value? A value is a principle or belief that a person or organization views as being of central importance. Simply stated, values are the things that matter most to you. Can that change over time? The short answer is yes, but it is a little more nuanced than that.

For some of us, values may be a gray area. You may have a general idea of what matters to you, like your family or your health, but if you've never really identified them, you may not have the words to truly define them. The first part of the framework, is to identify your values. Identifying values can feel like a big feat. Some of my clients have hesitated to do this exercise because they were afraid to pick something because they assumed they must stick to it, as if it would be written in stone. They were worried that they wouldn't be able to change their minds and that they were committing to something permanently. But the framework is an evolution, not a one-time exercise that has to be perfect.

When I do workshops with leaders within organizations or teams and coaching sessions with individuals or groups, we always start with identifying our individual values. We put words to them. Then we can start to understand what they mean and further define them.

It is not uncommon to be in a workshop or small group where multiple people share similar values. For instance, the value of impact is often listed out as a core value. But what impact means to one person may be totally different than what it means to another person.

In that same vein, what the core value of impact means to you this year could evolve to something else next year or even next month. So yes, values can change over time. But what I find most often, and even in my own experience, is that it's less the value and more the meaning of the value that changes over time. The word may stay the same, but how it looks like in your life can change. I love this—remember, we are learning, we are growing, and we are evolving. You can change a core value or just change the meaning of what living that value looks like in your life.

Through the process of trial and error, I now find that doing a Values Check-In exercise every ninety days is most effective. Do this to check in with your values to see if they are being met, and also to check in to see if anything has changed. In the Values Worksheet, there's a space to write down your secondary values, the ones that didn't make the list the first time. Sometimes I find that people combine two values and name it something new or promote a secondary value to a core value because it has become more important. And in that way, your values have evolved.

Yes, values can change over time. In my own experience and with my clients, it is more like refining your values to get to the right ones, evolving the definition or the way they show up, or updating them as you continue to grow.

SHOULD I HAVE BOTH PERSONAL AND WORK VALUES?

The next question that we'll explore came from a workshop with a senior leader and their direct reports. We were doing a values exercise where individuals identified their values as part of their team meeting, and before we started, a participant asked me whether they should have both personal and work values.

This is an important question and one that I think stems from the "separation of work and life" mentality that has been drilled into us for decades. Or rather, the balance of work and life. I don't believe in work-life balance, but I do believe in setting boundaries that prioritize what matters most (hint: your values).

The concept of separating work and life has been something that societal messaging has instilled for some time. More recently, we've seen some integration of work life and home life during and following the COVID-19 pandemic. However, the dichotomy of work and life has been present for decades. It is very interesting, and probably very American, that work gets the callout and life is just everything else.

Depending on our identities and our life experiences, we may find work either more or less safe than our home environment. This can be physical, mental, or psychological. People in marginalized groups especially may need to protect themselves in environments they don't know or trust yet. For many people, there is a difference in who they can safely be at work and who they are outside of work. Some leaders may feel like they need to separate values inside and outside of work.

So, back to the question: "Should you have personal and work values?"

You are a whole human, so I think you should have one set of core values. I do think that some of your values may show up differently in different aspects of your life, but the work and non-work

frequently asked questions

activities are both part of your life. Your life should have one set of core values.

I know you don't have time to have separate work and life values. I'm not going to tell you to double your work and manage two separate lists of values. Instead, I want you to center the things that you need and you value. One you, one core set of values.

For instance, if you have a value of creativity, how does that show up in different aspects of your life? At work that may mean that you give yourself thinking, brainstorming, or innovation time to deliberate and solve problems creatively. In other parts of your life, it may mean going to an art class or spending time journaling every day.

One struggle that has come up for some of my coaching clients is the pressure of putting values on their list. Sometimes this is driven by the values they think they should have.

One of my clients had family connection on her list of core values, and as she went through her iterations of values, she took it out. She mentioned that she had put it on there because, if she didn't have it, then what was she, a psychopath? Especially as a woman, she was supposed to care for others all the time, right? And what does that say about her as a person if she doesn't have "family" or something similar on her values set?

The same can be said for some clients thinking they should have a certain value on their list because it is a company value. What does that say about them, they don't have some of the same values as the company values? Would that mean that they don't belong here? That they don't care about the same things as everyone else? Would it show that they're less committed or less than in some way? It sometimes feels like that.

I go back to our meaning of values. A value is a principle or belief that a person or organization views as being of central importance. The things that matter most to you. So what matters most to you?

Not what matters most to other people, not what matters most to the company that you work for, not what matters most to someone that is sitting next to you in a workshop. What matters most to you? You, as a whole person.

acknowledgments

I'm so grateful to be in the position to write a second book, surrounded by support of family, friends, and clients.

Thank you to my family for being my biggest fans. There's nothing like getting a phone call from your parents to talk about that week's podcast topic or being asked by your child how your writing is going. Thank you for always supporting me!

Thank you to Lauren Marie Fleming, who continues to inspire me through telling the stories that need to be told, for believing in my story, and for coaching me through my first and second books. My author journey wouldn't exist without you.

Thank you to my beta readers who offered their time and gave me such thoughtful feedback. It really helped shape this book and the impact it will have. Thank you so much to Tara, Marilyn, Liz, Kate, Maddy, Jeannie, and Rita! You made this book better and more actionable.

Thank you to The Catch Group team: Tena, Ilektra, and Samantha. Your partnerships mean everything to me personally and professionally. I would not be able to live my values of growth, development, and advocacy without you.

Thank you to Amber Robidou for being the best rowing coach, for supporting me in my on-the-water rowing journey, and for the integral feedback on all things rowing in this book. All mistakes in the book are mine!

Thank you to Renae who encouraged me to write this book (and the next!).

To my students at Southern Methodist University, you inspire me daily. I know you'll do great things to make the world of work a better place for leaders and organizations.

Thank you to every leader who has shared their values journey with me. Your leadership belongs here. You are making huge impacts. Keep going and get on the boat!

references

1. O'Reilly, C. A., Chatman, J., & Caldwell, D. F. (1991). People and organizational culture: A profile comparison approach to assessing person-organization fit. *Academy of Management Journal, 34*(3), 487–516.
2. Brown, B.(2021). *Atlas of the heart: Mapping meaningful connection and the language of human experience.* Random Ho use.
3. O'Reilly, C.A ., & Pfeffer, J. (2000). *Hidden Value: How Great Companies Achieve Extraordinary Results with Ordinary People.* Harvard Business School Press.
4. George, G., Sleeth, R.G., & Siders, M.A . (1999). Organizing culture: Leader roles, behaviors, and reinforcement mechanisms. *Journal of Business and Psychology, 13,* 545–560.
5. Extreme. (1990). *Extreme II: Pornograffitti.* A&M Records.
6. Nygaard, A., Biong, H., Silkoset, R. et al. (2017). Leading by example: Values-based strategy to instill ethical conduct. *Journal of Business Ethics 145,* 133–139.
7. O'Reilly, C., Cao, X., & Sull, D. (2023). CEO personality: The cornerstone of organizational culture? *Group & Organization Management, 0*(0).
8. Brown, V.R ., & Paulus, P. (2002). Making group brainstorming more effective: Recommendations from an associative memory perspective. *Current Directions in Psychological Science 11*(6), 208–212.
9. Carson, J.B ., Tesluk, P.E ., & Marrone, J.A . (2007). Shared leadership in teams: An investigation of antecedent conditions and performance. *The Academy of Management Journal 50*(5), 1217–1234.
10. Donovan, R. (2023, April 12). *Are meetings making you less productive?* Stack Overflow Blog. https://stackoverflow.blog/2023/04/12/are-meetings-making-you-less-productive/
11. Eigel, L. (Host). (2023, November 22). Have better meetings and do less with Yari Ising (No. 135) [Audio podcast episode]. In *You Belong in the C-Suite.* The Catch Group.
12. Horton, A. P. (2024, February 18). *The ultimate guide for millennial managers working with Gen Z.* Fast Company. https://www.fastcompany.

13. com/91030423/the-ultimate-guide-for-millennial-managers-working-with-gen-z
13. Ben-Hur, S., & Kinley, N. (2016). Intrinsic motivation: The missing piece in changing employee behavior. *Perspectives for Managers 192*, 1–4.
14. Buffie, N. (2016, September 23). *The culture of overwork: A uniquely American phenomenon*. Center for Economic and Policy Research. https://cepr.net/the-culture-of-overwork-a-uniquely-american-phenomenon/.
15. Eigel, L. (Host). (2022, November 30). Belonging and advocacy with Amanda Knox (No. 88) [Audio podcast episode]. In *You Belong in the C-Suite*. The Catch Group.
16. Bell, K. (2015, August 27). *3 common problems with employee recognition programs*. Helios HR. https://www.helioshr.com/blog/2015/08/3-common-problems-with-employee-recognition
17. Porterfield, A. (Host). (2022, February). *Thriving as an introvert in an extrovert career* (No. 434) [Audio podcast episode]. In *Online Marketing Made Easy*. Amazon Music.
18. Berg, S.M . (2022). *Swing: Elite leadership for high performance teams*. Whithorn Press.

www.ingramcontent.com/pod-product-compliance
Lightning Source LLC
LaVergne TN
LVHW041941070526
838199LV00051BA/2864